Infomedia
in
HIGHER EDUCATION

Infomedia in HIGHER EDUCATION

AMJAD ALI

M.A., M.C.S., Ph.D. (L.I. & Sc.)

Ess Ess Publications

4837/24, Ansari Road, Darya Ganj,
New Delhi-110002
✆ : 23260807
Fax : 23274173
E-mail: essess@del3.vsnl.net.in

First Published 2004

ISBN : 81-7000-383-0

Price : Rs. 475/-

Published by :

Ess Ess Publications

4837/24, Ansari Road, Darya Ganj,
New Delhi - 110 002
Phone : 23260807
Fax : 23274173
E-mail : essess@del3.vsnl.net.in

Laser Typesetting:

Mukesh Graphics

L-2/8, DDA Market,
Mangolepuri, New Delhi
Ph. : 27924405

Printed at

Mehra Offset Press

Dedicated to
the Revered Memory of my Father

Haji Ghulam Hussain

Preface

Education has always been the basic need of mankind. It comes through instructions based on materials and methods. Information is the prime resource for instruction whether imparted verbally or through some other means. The utility of information largely depends upon the way of its presentation and also the perception process of man.

Technology brought crucial changes in the way of generating and acquiring of knowledge. It has great potential for education and research. Perhaps no other profession in the world has gained in so short a time than the education and information science. The emergence of audiovisuals, computer, CD ROM materials and Internet has revolutionized these professions.

As a result of advancements, new forms of learning are taking place now. Books are being actively substituted and even replaced by the products of information technology, specially, CD ROMs containing information in text, graphics, multimedia etc. The most important change during the last few years is the growing use of Internet for education, research and reference. In education sector, the shift from page to screen, which was once a fantasy is approaching reality. Higher education is no exception.

This book incorporates the historical development of educational media and the latest trends in digital technology being applied for collection, storage, management and dissemination of information. It is intended to meet the specific requirements of the students of library and information science, librarians, information professionals, educators and media managers.

I would like to thank all my well-wishers for their encouragement to carry out this work and the publisher for the interest and unstinted cooperation in publication of the book.

The work will be considered amply rewarded if the book

meets the expectations and requirements of those for whom it is meant. Any criticism and suggestions for further improvement will be gratefully acknowledged and highly appreciated.

Amjad Ali

140, Nai Abadi,

Kela Nagar, Aligarh-202 002

amjad_alig@yahoo.co.in

List of Abbreviations and Acronyms Used

AACR	Anglo American Cataloguing Rules
AAFT	Asian Academy of Film and Television
ACP	Audio Cassette Player
ACR	Audio Cassette Recorder
ACRL	Association of College and Research Libraries
AGLIS	Association of Government Librarians and Information Specialists
AIIMS	All India Institute of Medical Sciences
AIR	All India Radio
AISLIC	Association of Special Libraries and Information Centres
AIU	Association of Indian Universities
ALA	American Library Association
AMU	Aligarh Muslim University
AVRC	Audio Visual Research Centre
AVTU	Audio Visual Telecasting Unit
B. Lib. Sc.	Bachelor of Library Science
BCD	British Council Division
BCL	British Council Library
BLIS	Bachelor of Library and Information Science
CAS	Current Awareness Service
CBFC	Central Board of Film Certification
CC	Colon Classification
CCC	Classified Cataloguing Code

CCF	Common Communication Format
CD	Compact Disk
CDC	Curriculum Development Committee
CD-ROM	Compact Disk Read Only Memory
CDS/ISIS	Computerized Documentation Systems/ Integrated Set of Information Systems
CEC	Consortium for Educational Communication
CEMCA	Commonwealth Educational Media Centre for the Asia
CIET	Central Institute of Educational Technology
COL	Commonwealth of Learning
CPC	Central Production Centre
CWC	Countrywide Classroom
DAT	Digital Audio Tape
DBIT	Desidoc Bulletin of Information Technology
DDC	Dewey Decimal Classification
DDE	Directorate of Distance Education
DECU	Development and Educational Communication Unit
DELNET	Developing Library Network
Dept.	Department
DESIDOC	Defence Science Information and Documentation Centre
DGAIR	Directorate General of All India Radio
DIET	District Institute of Educational Technology
DPS	Delhi Public School
DRTC	Documentation Research and Training Centre
DST	Department of Science and Technology
DTP	Desk Top Publishing

DU	Delhi University
DVD	Digital Versatile Disk
EI	Educational International
E-mail	Electronic Mail
EMC	Educational Media Centre
ET	Educational Television
EMPC	Electronic Media Production Centre
EMRC	Educational Media Research Centre
ERNET	Education and Research Network
ET	Education Technology
ET&T	Electronic Trade and Technology
ETV	Educational Television
HDTV	High Definition Television
FAQ	Frequently Asked Questions
Fig	Figure
H/W	Hardware
IBM	International Business Machines
ICMR	Indian Council of Medical Research
IFLA	International Federation of Library Associations
IFTRC	International Film and Television Research Centre
IGNCA	Indira Gandhi National Centre for the Arts
IGNOU	Indira Gandhi National Open University
IIMC	Indian Institute of Mass Communication
IIT	Indian Institute of Technology
ILA	Indian Library Association
INSDOC	Indian National Scientific Documentation Centre
ILMS	Integrated Library Management System
IMC	Instructional Media Centre

INFLIBNET	Information and Library Network
INSAT	Indian National Satellite
INTACH	Indian National Trust for Cultural Heritage
ILMS	Integrated Library Management Software
ISBD	International Standard Bibliographic Description
ISRO	Indian Space Research Organization
IT	Information Technology
JMI	Jamia Millia Islamia
KWIC	Key Word in Context
KWOC	Key Word out of Context
LAN	Local Area Network
LCD	Liquid Crystal Display
LCLSH	Library of Congress List of Subject Headings
LEO	Low Earth Orbits
LIS	Library and Information Science
MS DOC	Microsoft Disk Operating System
M. Lib. Sc.	Master of Library Science
MARC	Machine Readable Catalogue
MC	Mass Communication
MCRC	Mass Communication Research Centre
MHRD	Ministry of Human Resource Development
MLIS	Master of Library and Information Science
NASSDOC	National Social Science Documentation Centre
NBM	Non Book Material
NCERT	National Council for Educational Research and Training
NEIF	National Education and Information Films
NEP	New Education Policy

NICEM	National Information Centre for Educational Media
NIE	National Institute of Education
NIEPA	National Institute for Educational Planning and Administration
NISSAT	National Information System for Science & Technology
NIVH	National Institute for the Visually Handicapped
NLM	National Library of Medicine
NOIDA	New Okhla Industrial Development Authority
NRLCCP	National Research Laboratory for Conservation of Cultural Property
NTSC	National Standards Television Committee
OPAC	Online Public Access Catalogue
PC/AT	Personal Computer Advanced Technology
PC/XT	Personal Computer Extended Technology
PCS	Personal Communication System
PE	Predominantly Educational
PGI	Post Graduate Institute
Ph.D.	Doctor of Philosophy
R&D	Research and Development
RIE	Regional Institute of Education
S/W	Software
SAC	Space Application Centre
SIET	State Institute of Educational Technology
SDI	Selective Dissemination of Information
SKUAST	Shere Kashmir University of Agricultural Sciences and Technology
TDCC	Training and Development Communication Channel

TIFAC	Technology Information Forecasting and Assessment Council
TOI	Times of India
TTTI	Technical Teachers Training Institute
TWT	Traveling Wave Tube
UDC	Universal Decimal Classification
UGC	University Grants Commission
UK	United Kingdom
UNDP	United Nations Development Programme
UNESCO	United Nation's Educational Scientific and Cultural Organization
UNO	United Nations Organization
UP	Uttar Pradesh
USIS	United States Information Service
UTs	Union territories
VCP	Video Cassette Player
VCR	Video Cassette Recorder
VHS	Video Home Service
WAN	Wide Area Network
Windows NT	Windows Networking
WWW	World Wide Web

CONTENTS

1. The Story of Paper ... 1
2. The Audiovisuals ... 9
3. The Electronic Media ... 15
4. Technology and Media in Education ... 31
5. Growth of Educational Media ... 49
6. Development of Media Collection ... 69
7. Organization of Library Resources ... 90
8. Information Sources and Systems ... 97
9. Networking and Resource Sharing ... 119
10. Organizational Needs of Media Libraries ... 130
11. Computer and the University Libraries ... 144
12 Internet, Intranet and Homepaging ... 173

Bibliography ... 197

Index ... 215

1

THE STORY OF PAPER

A major breakthrough in the history of mankind was the transformation of man from *Homo Sapien to Homo febra*– a man who thinks. The records of thinking were preserved by one generation for the other and thus passed on to posterity. What we have today is, undoubtedly, the result of thousands of years of thinking, experimentation and rethinking? The quantum of know-how increased in geometrical proportions. There were darker times too as many civilizations got devastated prematurely. But despite all the setbacks, the human race continued to grow and multiply the available knowledge.

We usually term the current rate of growth of knowledge as Information Revolution and consider it a contemporary phenomenon but its roots are there in history. H.Y. Sharda Prasad observes "The Information Revolution did not start in our century. It began when the hunter painted pictures of animals on wails of his cave. It took a step forward when speech was invented and further when early societies carved symbols first on stone, then on pottery, papyrus, palm leaf, birch back, cloth and paper to record individual impressions." ('The Mainstream, Annual 1993).

Different kind of materials; stones, clay tablets, leaves, cloth; parchment; vellum, etc. have been used for the purpose of preserving the acquired knowledge depending upon the availability of the materials and man's capability to use them. The rate of shifting from one material to the other has been very slow and in consonance with the transition in the society as a whole. The invention of paper from papyrus in Egypt around two thousand years ago was perhaps the biggest gift to mankind. For centuries, paper made all forms of learning and research possible.

Paper has been used for the longest time as the basic material for written communication and the dissemination of information comparing with stones, clay tablet, tree leave, cloth, and. It is one of the most widely used media, which dominated the scene of learning for the last many centuries. Paper coupled with the moveable types invented in the 15th century accelerated the rate of growth of the recorded knowledge. It was a cheaper and easily available medium and even mass production was not difficult. From this invention onwards, the quantum of publication was so high that whatever number of books the whole of Europe could have brought out till the 15th century was produced within a year of this invention. Paper became an indispensable reality in every civilized society ever since.

The word paper is derived from the name of the reedy plant papyrus, which grows abundantly along the Nile River in Egypt. In ancient times, the fibrous layers within the stem of this plant were removed, placed side by side, and crossed at right angles with another set of layers similarly arranged. The sheet so formed was dampened and pressed. Upon drying, the glue like sap of the plant, acting as an adhesive, cemented the layers together. Complete defibring, an indispensable element in modern papermaking, did not occur in the preparation of papyrus sheets. Papyrus was the most widely used writing material in ancient times, and many papyrus records still survive.

The history of papermaking can be traced to about AD 105, when Ts'ai Lun, an official attached to the Imperial court of China, created a sheet of paper using mulberry and other bast fibrés along with fishnets, old rags, and hemp waste. In its slow travel westward, the art of papermaking reached Samarkand, in Central Asia, in 751; and in 793 the first paper was made in Baghdad during the time of Harun ar-Rashid, with the golden age of Islamic culture that brought papermaking to the frontiers of Europe.

The Arabs got papermaking 600 years later as one of the spoils of war. The Central Asian city of Samarkand was fighting the Chinese and captured a number of prisoners, two of whom were papermakers who were released in exchange for teaching the Arabs how to make paper. The Arabs wasted no time in improving papermaking techniques - they were probably the first to make paper from linen - and they spread the techniques throughout the Middle East and into Spain.

By the 14th century a number of paper mills existed in Europe, particularly in Spain, Italy, France, and Germany. The invention of printing in the 1450s brought a vastly increased demand for paper. Through the 18th century the papermaking process remained essentially unchanged, with linen and cotton rags furnishing the basic raw materials. Paper mills were increasingly plagued by shortages; in the 18th century they even advertised and solicited publicly for rags. It was evident that a process for utilizing a more abundant material was needed.

At the time when Gutenberg produced his first Bible around 1456, Europe was still predominantly using parchment and vellum for printing, rather than paper. Parchment is the skin of a sheep or goat that' is prepared for writing; vellum is a fine parchment made from the skins of calves, lambs or kids. Gutenberg printed several copies of his Bible on parchment; to print just one, he had to use the skins of 300 sheep. Now with that kind of resource demand, obviously there were not enough goats and sheep and calves in Europe to allow the mass production of books. So here was this grand new technology - the printing press - and no way to realize its potential, until entrepreneurs saved the day by improving and expanding the technology of making paper from linen rags. At first, paper was called "cloth parchment."

Book production increased as a result of the easy availability of paper. Newspapers started appearing in the late 1600s and early 1700s. Newspapers, and the increased communication they offered, began to affect the conduct of government and commerce. Newspapers played an important role in spreading political information in the pre-Revolutionary and Revolutionary period and also in education.

Booksellers in the Middle Ages seldom had many ready-made books in his shop. They were copied down by hand which took a lot of time and resources that everybody was not able to afford. It was done by simply borrowing the first few pages of the book and taking them home for copying. These pages were usually returned before borrowing the next few pages. There's a story, perhaps apocryphal, about Gutenberg's financial partner - when he offered 20 identical copies of the Bible to a bookseller in Paris, he was quickly forced to flee for his life. People were certain that the only explanation for this bizarre occurrence was that he was in league with the Devil.

The moveable types allowed lower cost of printing books on paper. Their subsequent availability, stimulated the foundation of new schools and universities. Because books were now more numerous, educational opportunities that were once restricted to the nobility and upper classes were now becoming somewhat more available to other classes in society, with dramatic increases in levels of education and literacy.

When changing from an oral culture, where everything is communicated in stories and the spoken word, to a literate culture, where people get their information by reading, one changes even such fundamentals as the process of thinking. Suddenly people don't have to carry all their knowledge in their heads. They don't have to develop elaborate ways of memorizing. They start to think in a more linear fashion because now they can work out on paper the complicated thought progressions that they hadn't been able to do in their heads.

The art world was also transformed by improvements in papermaking. Previously, artists had to practice their techniques and develop their drawing abilities on canvasses that they painted over and over again, so most paintings were actually lost - hidden under layers and layers of new paint. When paper became available as a cheap type of "canvas," artists could go wild practicing their sketching, and now these sketches could be saved. For the first time, drawing became an important art form in itself.

The breakthrough in papermaking technology fueled a huge expansion in business that eventually led to the development of the modern corporation, which was unable to function without tremendous supplies of paper. The paper industry in the 1850s crated changes so far-reaching that it was one of the transformation factors in the developing the nations. Not the least revolutionary change was the astounding drop in newsprint prices that advances in papermaking technology allowed.

Throughout the eighteenth century, there was an intense search in Europe and the U.S. for a new fiber source of paper. Contests were held, universities offered prizes, and inventors and laboratories worked feverishly to come up with a new source for paper. Inventors would often print a book on their newly-invented paper that described how the paper was made. And it ended up with books printed on paper made from asbestos, straw, swamp grass, marsh mallow, and esparto dune grass from certain beaches in Spain. The first patent for a paper using deinked waste paper as pat of its fiber source was issued in 1800 in London. It was not until the 1840s that the initial development of the papermaking machine in England and experiments in groundwood pulping in Germany and Nova Scotia enabled the commercial production of paper.

In 1800 a book was published that launched development of practical methods for manufacturing paper from wood pulp and other vegetable pulps. Several major pulping processes were gradually developed that relieved the paper industry of dependency upon cotton and linen rags and made modern large-scale production possible. These developments followed two distinct pathways. In one, fibres and fibre fragments were separated from the wood structure by mechanical means; and in the other, the wood was exposed to chemical solutions that dissolved and removed lignin and other wood components, leaving cellulose fibre behind.

Prior to the invention of the paper machine, paper was made one sheet at a time by dipping a frame or mold with a screened bottom into a vat of stock. Lifting the mold allowed the water to drain, leaving the sheet on the screen. The sheet was then pressed and dried. The size of a single sheet was limited to the size of frame and mold that a man could lift from a vat of stock.

Although modern inventions and engineering have transformed an ancient craft into a highly technical industry, the basic operations in papermaking remain the same to this day. The steps in the process are as follows: (1) a suspension of cellulosed fibre is prepared by beating it in water so that the fibres are thoroughly separated and saturated with water; (2) the paper stock is filtered on a woven screen to form a matted sheet of fiber; (3) the wet sheet is pressed and compacted to squeeze out a large proportion of water; (4) the remaining water is removed by evaporation; and (5) depending upon use requirements, the dry paper sheet is further compressed, coated, or impregnated.

The cell walls of all plants contain fibers of cellulose, an organic material known to chemists as a linear polysaccharide. It constitutes about one-third of the structural material of annual plants and about one-half that of perennial plants. Cellulose fibres have high strength and durability. They are readily wetted by water, exhibiting considerable swelling when saturated, and are hygroscopic—i.e., they absorb appreciable amounts of water when exposed to the atmosphere. Even in the wet state, natural cellulose fibres show no loss in strength. It is the combination of these qualities with strength and flexibility that makes cellulose of unique value for paper manufacture.

Cotton and linen fibres, derived from textile and garment mill cuttings; cotton linters (the short fibers recovered from the processing of cottonseed after the separation of the staple fibre); flax fibres; and clean, sorted rags are still used for those grades of paper in which maximum strength, durability, and permanence, as well as fine formation, colour, texture, and feel, are required. These properties are attributed to the greater fineness, length, and purity of rag fibre as compared with most wood pulp. Rag papers are used extensively for bank note and security certificates; life insurance policies and legal documents, for which permanence is of prime importance; technical papers, such as tracing paper, vellums, and reproduction papers; high-grade bond letterheads, which must be impressive in appearance and texture; lightweight specialties such as cigarette, carbon, and Bible papers; and high-grade stationery, in which beauty, softness, and fine texture are desired.

Rags are received at the paper mill and once cooked, the rags are washed, then mechanically beaten. The beating shortens the fiber, increases the swelling action of water to produce a softened and plastic fibre, and fibrillates or frays the fibre to increase its surface area. All of these actions contribute to better formation of the paper sheet, closer contact between fibres, and the formation of interfiber bonding that gives the paper strength and coherence.

Since cellulose fibre is a major constituent of the stems of plants, a vast number of plants represent potential sources of paper; many of these have been pulped experimentally. A rather substantial number of plant sources have been used commercially, at least on a small scale and at various times and places. Indeed, the use of cereal straws for paper predates the use of wood pulp and is widely practiced today throughout the world, although on a relatively small scale of production. Because many parts of the world are deficient in forests, the development of the paper industry in these areas appears to depend to a considerable degree upon the use of annual plants and agricultural fibres.

Because of the abundance of bamboo in Southeast Asia, where increased production of paper is greatly needed, much interest has been displayed in bamboo pulp development. The growing cycle of bamboo is favourable, for the culms can be harvested without destroying the root system. Under ideal conditions of soil fertility and moisture, an established stand of bamboo probably would produce more fibre per hectare (or acre) per year than any other plant. Wild bamboo, however, is difficult to harvest and transport economically; so far, the interest in it has not been translated into any large-scale production. Pulp mills make use of bamboo in India, Thailand, and the Philippines. Considerable quantities of bamboo pulp are said to be made in China, but details are lacking

In the ancient time, the media of communication had durability but lacked portability. This was achieved with the invention of paper. Further, the celluloid medium contributed in reduction of size of documents and made mass transfer of information possible through microfilms, microfiches and ultra fiches. This new medium also presented a different kind of material for understanding of reality and that was in the form of motion pictures.

2

The Audiovisuals

It is often said that a picture is worth a thousand words as it may communicate a huge mass of ideas, and mean differently to different people. Photography emerged as an appropriate medium for such presentation, which coupled with the technology of sound proved to be the greatest and the most significant form for presentation of ideas.

The present day photography is the result of the early observations by alchemists and chemists based on the action of light on the photosensitive materials. The technique developed towards the end of the 18th century when the demand for the pictures grew. A major advancement in photography took place with substitution of glass for paper as a carrier for the light sensitive material. In 1851, once the manufacture of photographic materials was established as a commercial industry, the photographic techniques followed steady growth. In 1012 Kodak Company introduced flat film in place of glass plates for making negatives. The technique was advantageous for manufacturers. A few years later, the development in new sensitizing dyes made it possible for preparing panchromatic materials of improved quality.

Radio emerged as one of the most potent media of mass communication since it made possible the transmission and reception of signals by means of electronic wave and without the use of connecting wires. Within a century of its invention radio has grown enormously going out of Marconi's workshop to a permanent fixture in almost all the homes the world over.

Eventually the industry came to recognize radio as a way of stimulating sales. By 1930, a magazine, Billboard was reporting that "sheet music and record dealers now consider radio a boon to their business, rather than a detriment." The magazine's initial radio coverage, a one-eighth-page section called Radio Entertainers that first appeared in 1928.

By 1930, the full-page Radio Entertainers section joined the front-cover list of Billboard's regularly covered entertainment businesses, which also included burlesque, skating rinks, rodeos, and, of course, popular songs. In those days, the magazine known as The Billboard was billed as "The Theatrical Digest And Show World Review." About that same time, stations' regular on-air personalities began to make news in Billboard, not just the visiting entertainers The radio business at that time was divided into independent and network-affiliated stations, and most programs aired in 15-minute blocks. Unlike today's focused, niche programming, a typical station's programming in 1932 was 62.9% music, 21.3% educational, 11.8% literature, 2.5% religion, and 1.5% "novelties," according to a study released that year.

Following the Japanese attack on Pearl Harbor and the start of U.S. involvement in World War II, Billboard's radio coverage focused on the medium's role in the war effort. That role was a vital one, since radio provided the country not only with news, but with public-service messages, entertainment, and much-needed morale boosting. In the war's first year, a typical NBC station aired 5,300 government announcements, 4,500 War Bond announcements, and 2,700 war-effort programs, for a total of 990 hours of war-related programming over and above news reports.

Many forms of presentations emerged and met extinction within a short life span of radio spreading over the last fifty years.

By 1975, the once-popular nostalgia format was fading. Radio Drama had been dead for more than a decade, and the disco format was "being studied based on the records played in the growing number of discotheques throughout. Since its development in 1895, the radio has long since been revolutionizing the world. It has become so common that it is very improbable that one could ever pass a day without coming into contact with radio in some shape or fashion. In the beginning, radios were the only form of entertainment other than family outings and live shows such as those seen on Broadway. However, it seems like radio has outlived its passion for the programs and evening news and now concentrates almost completely on music.

The radio not only revolutionized the world but also created a new form of entertainment and education that will more than likely carry on for many centuries to come. Perhaps this invention was soon able to travel through space, collect tremendous amounts of data from the universe, and spell out for us the reality of new frontiers waiting to be explored. Truly the radio will live on forever.

Photography coupled with sound heralded a new era in of communication of ideas. It followed the invention and application of a variety of technologies for recording and presentation of information. It began with the art of sight and sound, which later transformed into tape slide shows. But with further improvements in synchronization of sound with the moving images, the present day cinematography took its birth.

The development in photography and cinematography brought significant changes in the world of learning. Now more sense organs were involved in the perception process. The human nature is so that the maximum of ones total knowledge is perceived through the senses of sight and sound and the new media of communication available as a result of these advancements exploited this potential of man to its full, facilitating learning at a higher speed and with a greater ease. The trend was on for about thirty years in India from the mid of the last century. The celluloid medium was primarily adopted for entertainment but soon it became equally popular in the academic circles. Film became the medium of instruction within fifty years of its existence.

Cinematographic film consists of a transparent flexible support or base on which is laid a photosensitive adhesive emulsion. They are now available in different widths ranging from 8 mm to 70 mm. The more the width the higher is the cost of the film. They are used for varied purposes depending upon the cost and the quality of the film. The super 8 mm is used very rarely as the infrastructure for production on this format is not generally available. But this is certainly the cheapest cinematographic medium available so far. The 16 mm film is used by most of the institutions for education and development. This has advantage over 8 mm because of comparatively higher resolution being suitable to be magnified on slightly larger screen.

Both the 8 mm and 16 mm films are used depending upon the size of the audience as well as the cost of the production involved. The 35 mm and 70 mm films are normally used for entertainment and commercial purposes. They are suitable for larger gatherings like the audience of feature films in cinema halls. The advertisement agencies produce ads on these formats. The advantage of their having larger width is that the picture contains very high resolution and does not blow up while magnified on larger screens. Sound for cinematographic films can be recorded magnetically or optically depending upon the circumstances.

Video is basically a picture and sound recording medium. It is also cheaper in Comparison to the cinematographic film. The great advantage of this medium is its instant playback facility. Video Productions are generally available on videotapes and videocassettes. Their width vary from super 8 mm to 2". VHS is the most suited format for home viewing and a small gathering. The formats of video are changing very fastly. In India, within a decade the production studios have witnessed reel to reel videotapes, 1" BCN, 3/4" U-

Matic in low and high band and currently the Betacam in 1/2". There is a possibility of shift of the medium to digital in the coming times since this format has certain advantages over the existing ones.

The audiovisual medium was used basically for entertainment purposes but its potential was soon recognized in the academic circles. Film became the medium of instruction. In India many institutions such as the Central Institute of Educational Technology (CIET), State Institutes of Educational Technology (SIETs) came into being apart from the Films Division and the National Films Development Corporation. The teaching and learning institutions too were attracted by the power of this medium. As a result, open universities with the multimedia approach to instruction were established. The University Grants Commission took special interest in popularizing education through the audio-visual media. Within a span of 9 years of inception of the UGC/INSAT/TV Project at the Mass Communication Research Centre in Jamia Millia Islamia, New Delhi, the number of media production centres, popularly known as the Educational Media Research Centres/Audio Visual Research Centres rose to 17 from only one in 1984.

Motion pictures are now available on cinematographic film as well as on video. Their basic and common characteristic is the movement of picture on the screen. The movement is achieved by running a film or video through a projector or player at a speed of 24 frames per second. The stills are recorded in a situation where all of them are comparatively similar and differ only at the point where movement has to be visualized. Motion pictures include silent and sound films as well. Nowadays, nearly all of them are being recorded in colour.

Motion pictures are being accepted increasingly by the academic circles as a learning aid as well as the medium for preservation of information. In India, we always need good instructional and enrichment films available in the international market. But there are hurdles in their import Even for the academic and research purposes. This requires urgent attention of all concerned so that motion picture can also be imported like books for the purpose of education and research. Moreover, just as there are renowned authors so are there well known film makers who have a series of worthwhile films to their credit and which could be an intrinsic part of every library.

Looking at the newer electronic media of audiovisuals, we find the difference quite visible. The audiovisual programs are being produced mainly on cassettes now which are becoming cheaper despite the fact that the human factor is involved in their production and that the human labour is becoming costlier everywhere in the world. It is worth mentioning here that British India Company started distribution of the same cassette in 1982 at the rat of Rs. 420 per cassette. Similarly, the price of the recorded cassettes is either decreasing or is stable. Computers, modems, discs, antennas, TV sets, VCRs/VCPs, nearly all the equipment and accessories used in the information storage and retrieval and based on the electronic devices are becoming cheaper. The main reason is the availability of improved technology based on Very Large Scale Integration (VLSI) and the mass production of electronic goods. The cost of audio visual programs too has gone down about 10 times with the adoption of video in place of celluloid. On celluloid, the shooting of sequences involved much pain and the result was known only after developing the prints whereas video offers instant playback facility. Thus, the wastage of efforts or resources is minimum in the electronic media of audiovisuals.

3

THE ELECTRONIC MEDIA

Paper has undoubtedly been the companion of learners and the main medium of communication of ideas for more time in comparison to any other medium. But the improved technology for storage and dissemination of information has made available a wide range of products that accommodate a fairly larger body of information. Reduction in size of documents by photographic process was one of the first measures in reducing the space required for housing information. All these discoveries were based on optics and chemical processes. The documents required utmost care in handling and preservation and it was almost impossible to preserve them beyond a few decades.

Computer is regarded as the greatest invention of all the times. It facilitates the storage, processing and distribution of information much easier with its vast memory speed and accuracy. The advancements in calculator, which was invented to carry out mathematical calculations led to the invention of computer.

A more visible change took place when calculators acquired the capability of processing textual data proceeded by the capacity to process information available in varied formats. Further improvements in computer design during the 1960s enabled the integration of text and graphics, a move that encouraged the development of computer based training programs. Such use was however limited, as programming was costly, slow and cumbersome, and the computing relied on a mainframe, or central computer to do all the work. The release of the first microcomputers during the late 1970s saw computing become more portable and affordable. Ease of use took a quantum leap with the introduction of the Apple Macintosh computer in 1984. Operation of the computer and its programs became more intuitive, largely as a result of research in the area of human-computer interaction.

The adoption of computers in the area of vocational training also increased, with some industries recognising that the technology offered benefits that were largely centred on efficiency gains. This was particularly the case in industries such as finance and insurance, manufacturing, health care, and the armed forces where training was a critical but costly component of operation. These types of organisations, with large staff numbers requiring training to an industry standard, or with staff located across national and international borders, found cost savings could be achieved by using technology to distribute training programs to the workplace, rather than bring staff to a central training centre. Computer programs could deliver training at a time and place convenient to all parties, provide flexibility in terms of progression and pace, generate and score tests, record all interaction between the learner and the system and produce detailed reports of this interaction. These attributes were welcomed in organisations where staff development programs were valued as a means of motivating staff and maintaining the standard of service. These programs are commonly based on competency standards that clearly define objectives, and set standards of performance that may be observed and measured against defined criteria.

The notion of providing training when it was needed to where it was needed was extended through the development of performance support systems. These systems allowed an employee to use a computer as both a tool and a tutor - the tutor would provide step by step assistance in the performance of specific computer related tasks, in much the same way as help "wizards" incorporated within many Microsoft products try to anticipate users needs in designing a new spreadsheet or database. Computer based training has also been a logical choice where there was substantial risk in allowing a novice to train in an operational environment. It is safer and more cost effective to allow the operator of a steel rolling mill to practice the procedure using a computer simulation, or a pilot to manage an engine failure without leaving the ground. Submariners crewing the Australian Navy's new Collins Class submarines were expected to develop a familiarity of the control systems prior to the vessels delivery, again through the use of computer simulations. Adoption of computers in education has not always met with similar success. The reasons are varied, and these will be discussed in the next section. Computers can be an asset in education, but the knowledge of appropriate applications, limitations and advantage needs to be clearly understood.

The electronic media has the capability to store, manipulate and transfer information in the form of text as well as audio visuals. It is also possible to combine both of them. Multimedia and hypermedia can be cited as examples. The electronic media is useful in learning both in a classroom situation or individually. It includes information networks and CD ROMs. The information is recorded electronically, hence greater speed, accuracy and memory is available to the users. It is presumed that within the coming decade, the electronic media will supersede all the available media for storage, management and dissemination of information. This will particularly affect the educational institutions as it is more effective and economic both in terms of money and time spent in learning. It will also affect the nature of classroom instruction. A new learning culture is in the offing which can be seen in the open system of education where attendance in class is not a prerequisite to earn a degree.

The advances in electronics and telecommunications brought newer technology capable of accommodating very large quantities of information in a very little space. Magnetic tapes, CD-ROMs, multimedia and hypermedia are a few examples. One CD-ROM can accommodate 3,00,000 pages of A4 size text that is equal to 10 full sets of the Encyclopedia Britannica spreading over 300 volumes containing approximately 1,000 pages each. The space required for storing one Compact Disc is negligible. One floor of a library stack normally accommodating around 30 volumes of books can easily hold 300 discs. Thus a double-faced library stack with 28 shelves is capable of storing materials equal to 25,20,00,000 pages or nearly 25,20,000 volumes of books. Further, the storage capacity may be doubled if the stacks are partitioned according to the size of the disc and not the size of books which require more space.CD ROMs have the capacity to record and display large amount of information through computer system. The information contained in them can be manipulated and produced in varied sequences. They are easy to consult and make the searches convenient. The Microsoft Corporation has come out with a set of two CD ROMs that contains information equal to about twenty encyclopedia and the information it holds can be searched through various options.

CD ROMs have an edge on print as well as online resources. On the one hand they save a lot of physical space required for their print counterpart while on the other hand they allow to work on huge resources independent of online connectivity that is far expensive. The increasing cost of Internet connectivity also suggests that CD ROM technology is more suited to education and research. Document in an ever-increasing number are being directly published, on CD ROMs without involving prints. Now experts believe that the shift from page to screen once a fantasy is approaching reality now. Students in many university use textbook that exist online. Similarly there are CD ROMs, which hold valuable academic information and are the only sources of information in certain areas of study like medicine and technology.

In the electronic media, search time has been reduced miraculously. Bulky reference tools like the Chemical Abstracts, Dissertation Index, Index to Higher Theses, encyclopedias and dictionaries, etc. can be searched within a fraction of a second by just pushing the keys of a computer. Further, the search is very easy as most of the databases are user friendly. Any of the related words can be taken as 'Search Term' and fed into the system for retrieval of information. This is followed by appearance of a detailed list of documents available on the same topic from which one can select the most relevant and pinpointed information and even download it in the memory of the computer or on auxiliary memory for future use. There are some restrictions. Words, which can create hindrance are debarred from the retrieval process. They are called stop words. This is achieved by maintaining a separate file for them.

Another advantage of electronic media is the updating of the reference tools. Unlike the printed medium, which requires repeating the whole mechanical process for improvement or updating, the information is updated instantly in the electronic media. This is achieved with the push of a button. In fact, the agencies dealing in the electronic sources of information enter into an agreement with the consumers. The same discs can be sent to the agencies and returned updated. Now, with the Electronic Mail facility, updating can be carried out instantly on line. 'This practically involves no time and saves expenditure as well. In the print as well as the celluloid, mass copying leads to deterioration of prints by way of generation loss. But in the electronic media, the same text can be generated again and again without any loss or deterioration in the quality of the original or its copy.

In a tropical country like India the fluctuation in temperature and humidity leads to deterioration in the quality of print as well as celluloid by way of chemical reactions. This process of degeneration goes on with the passage of time. It is very difficult to maintain quality of print beyond a century and of celluloid beyond a decade. The solution lies to some extent in erection of specialized dehumidified chambers and providing air conditioners but this too is not practicable for many other reasons such as frequent breakdowns in supply of electricity and the huge expenditure involved.

Role of Digital Communication

In the early times, it was smoke that communicated meanings to the responders at the other end. Then it took the form of written messages. Now information is transferred to the other places in a number of ways. The telecommunication has brought a revolution in the ways of sending messages at distant places virtually without involving any considerable amount of time.

Fiber optics communicates data in digital form and is a very reliable channel for communication of huge quantity of data. A single glass fiber is thinner than the size of a human hair and it can transmit all the characters in dozens of books of the same size across the country in a single second. Such a quantity of information will normally take about 21 hours to send over a copper telephone line. Fiber Optic technology is a cutting edge method of transmitting information over great distances (150 km without using a repeater) using pulses of light.

Fiber optic technology sends data without electricity through a conductor. Instead of electrical signals, modulated light is used to quickly transmit data over great distances through an insulated glass Fiber-type material.

Fiber optics is currently the best long distance communication method because it provides much faster data transfer speeds when compared to traditional interconnection media such as copper wire. The signal cannot be disrupted by outside sources like electricity, rain, humidity, or other things that tend to damage conventional copper wire signals. Fiber Optic Cables are ideal for volatile environments because there is no fear of damage should they break like there is with traditional copper wiring.

Optical Fiber is lightweight compared to copper cabling because it is a thin glass strand and has huge bandwidth because information travels along the Fiber at the speed of light. Thousands of fibers can be fit in the same amount of space as required for one cable. The developments in fiber optics suggest that the future cost of broad band transmission capability will be within the reach of small organizations and individuals.

Another significant mode of communication that revolutionized the process of information exchange is the satellite. Satellite Communication has turned the entire world into a global village. Satellites relay or transmit information such as TV, phone, weather, military intelligence, and data. Communications satellites provide a worldwide link. In 1960, Echo 1 was launched becoming the first communications satellite. The primitive Echo 1 was an inflatable metallic sphere with instruments that bounced radio signals back to earth. Two years later, Telstar 1 became the first active communications satellite. These satellites orbit the earth at a relatively low altitude. This made them difficult to track and not very suitable for communication. Active satellites receive, amplify, and retransmit signals to different locations. Telstar 1 was responsible for the relay of the first live television broadcast across the Atlantic Ocean.

Perhaps the first person to carefully evaluate the various technical options in satellite communications *and* evaluate the financial prospects was John R. Pierce of AT&T's Bell Telephone Laboratories who, in a 1954 speech and 1955 article, elaborated the utility of a communications "mirror" in space, a medium-orbit "repeater" and a 24-hour-orbit "repeater." In comparing the communications capacity of a satellite, which he estimated at 1,000 simultaneous telephone calls, and the communications capacity of the first trans-atlantic telephone cable (TAT-1), which could carry 36 simultaneous telephone calls at a cost of 30-50 million dollars, Pierce wondered if a satellite would be worth a billion dollars. After the 1957 launch of Sputnik I, many considered the benefits, profits, and prestige associated with satellite communications. In 1965, Intelsat 1, nicknamed "early bird", became the first commercial geosynchronous satellite. It was launched by COMSAT. Currently a network of 19 Intelsat satellites provide instantaneous communications throughout the world. The current generation Intelsat 8, can handle 22,500 two-way phone calls and three color television broadcasts simultaneously. Recent advances in electronic equipment could increase the number of telephone circuitry to 112,500. There are also communication satellites launched by individual countries, organizations, and businesses in orbit. Within the last ten years the first direct broadcast satellites were launched.

Weather forecasting has undergone a revolution because of the availability of pictures from geostationary meteorological satellites—pictures we see every day on television. All of these are important aspects of the space age, but satellite communications has probably had more effect than any of the rest on the average person. Satellite communications is also the only truly commercial space technology. By the time EARLY BIRD was launched, communications earth stations already existed in the United Kingdom, France, Germany, Italy, Brazil, and Japan. Further negotiations in 1963 and 1964 resulted in a new international organization, which would ultimately assume ownership of the satellites and responsibility for management of the global system. On August 20, 1964, agreements were signed which created the International Telecommunications Satellite Organization. By the end of 1965, EARLY BIRD had provided 150 telephone "half- circuits" and 80 hours of television service. The INTELSAT II series was a slightly more capable and longer-lived version of EARLY BIRD. Much of the early use of the COMSAT/INTELSAT system was to provide circuits for the NASA Communications Network (NASCOM). The INTELSAT III series was the first to provide Indian Ocean coverage to complete the global network. This coverage was completed just days before one half billion people watched APOLLO 11 land on the moon on July 20, 1969.

In 1965, ABC proposed a domestic satellite system to distribute television signals. 1. In early 1976 AT&T and COMSAT launched the first of the COMSTAR series. These satellites were used for voice and data, but very quickly television became a major user. By the end of 1976 there were 120 transponders available over the U.S., each capable of providing 1500 telephone channels or one TV channel. Very quickly the "movie channels" and "super stations" were available to most Americans. The dramatic growth in cable TV would not have been possible without an inexpensive method of distributing video.

The basic communications component of the satellite was the traveling-wave-tube (TWT).These had been invented in England by Rudoph Kompfner, but they had been perfected at Bell Labs by Kompfner and J. R. Pierce. All three early satellites used TWTs built by a Bell Labs alumnus.

In 1965, when EARLY BIRD was launched, the satellite provided almost 10 times the capacity of the submarine telephone cables for almost 1/10th the price. Satellites are still competitive with cable for point-to-point communications, but the future advantage may lie with fiber-optic cable. Satellites still maintain two advantages over cable: they are more reliable and they can be used point-to-multi-point (broadcasting). Cellular telephone systems have risen as challenges to all other types of telephony. It is possible to place a cellular system in a developing country at a very reasonable price. Long-distance calls require some other technology, but this can be either satellites or fiber-optic cable. Cellular telephony has brought us a new technological system, the personal communications system (PCS). In the fully developed PCS, the individual would carry his telephone with him. This telephone could be used for voice or data and would be usable anywhere. Several companies have committed themselves to providing a version of this system using satellites in low earth orbits (LEO).

The inherent "broadcast" nature of satellite communications has made direct-broadcast a recurrent theme—yet one never brought to fruition. Each year from 10-20 communications satellites are launched making the process of communication of information more easy and effective day by day.

The confluence of satellite and multimedia resulted in making the communication technology available at an unimaginably lower cost to the betterment of the common man although it originated in labs for scientific researchers. Now, Internet services are primarily based on these technologies.

Multimedia represents the convergence between computers, digital video, digital audio and sound synthesis. It has initially culminated the re-evaluation of the ways in which we communicate information combining still and moving images, sound, text and audio. Day to day applications of multimedia can be visualized considering information activities around us. Multimedia is being increasingly adopted for education and training, reference, business, entertainment etc.

Multimedia is widely acknowledged as an environment with great potentiality for education. It is able to assist both the people and teachers in new ways since for teacher it provides a means of putting across information and ideal and for students it can represent a one-to-one teaching environment which moves at the required pace.

Distribution of multimedia lessons, lectures and courseware on CD ROM or CD-1 discs adds another dimension to multimedia in education providing a vehicle of information to the students to take home. Its potential is enormous for the rural communities and isolated geographical regions where schools are inaccessible. The Open University teaching will certainly depend more upon the means and methods presented by advances in multimedia in the time to come.

As projected in the past we have now libraries without space. An information specialist sitting comfortably at his place of work just connecting his computer can establish contact with the desired number of foreign databases and an interaction can follow for the desired information. These services are being offered now on commercial basis too. The information thus selected can be downloaded on computer for further use.

Pupils traveled long distances in the past in search of information. Now information is knocking at their doors. The electronic devices have made it possible to transfer information at the speed of light. Pictures and sounds too are being transmitted from one place to the other. What is important today, is the selection of information and its dissemination for application. The quantum of information available is so much that everybody can have enough to learn individually. This is because of the coordination of efforts at the global level and presentation of this vast amount of information in a way that makes it convenient for the users to determine what is relevant to their needs.

Many academic institutions in the West have made database search an integral part of their educational process. Now thanks to the power of CD-ROM technology, information on nearly all the disciplines of education is available within reach of virtually every academic institution, its teachers, students and researchers. One can search as broadly, as deeply and as long as he or she wishes. The Indian National Scientific Documentation Centre is providing professional expertise in this regard to the academic and research institutions in India. Some other agencies like the Videsh Sanchar Nigam, the National Informatics Centre and the Faxon Informatics, Bangalore also coordinate in subscribing to these services. The data available from these agencies reveals steady growth in demand of the On-Line Information Services by the academic institutions in India.

The electronic media allows portability as well as durability. Information recorded digitally can last for centuries virtually with no effect of humidity, dust or temperature. The quality of recording is not affected because the information is not recorded on the surface but within the medium itself. The electronic media seems to be ideal for preservation of manuscripts and other valuable records. There are two ways of recording from paper on to the digital media- one is the transfer of text page wise and the other is that the contents of rare manuscripts are entered word by word. Thus, not only the life of the documents increases but also they can be retrieved rapidly and made available to the researchers.

The present situation has become an ideal one for adoption of Internet as in the words of Bill Gates "For the first time, all kinds of information-numbers, text, sound, video-can be put into a digital form that any computer can now store, process and forward. For the first time, standard hardware combined with a standard software platform has created economies of scale that make powerful computing solutions available extensively to all kinds of companies" (Business @ the speed of thought: Penguin Books: London (1999).

The Internet

Internet has emerged as the most powerful medium for storage and retrieval of information. It works round the clock and connects every nook and corner of the world. With an unprecedented growth in the quantum of knowledge worldwide and easy accessibility, Internet has become an unavoidable necessity for every institution of higher learning and research.

Internet is continuously growing internationally. Within a short span of ten years, its services have been spread among all the nations of the world. In 1991 it was within reach of 73 countries but within four years of its existence Internet reached 148 countries. The number of Internet users is also increasing tremendously as they are almost doubled after every two years. In the meanwhile Internet widened its scope. Now it is used for storage, manipulation and dissemination of textual data as well as the multimedia.

Internet became more popular by its feature of the World Wide Web. In 1991, Tim Berners-Lee, a young scientist working in European Particle Physics Laboratory (CERN) produced Internet's first browser. According to him, "the dream behind the Web is of a common information space in which we communicate by sharing information.' By its application, someone could scan every document or photo or video on the net. It gave an opportunity to share the resources by individuals and organizations on the basis of mutual understanding. In the past ten years, it has been so popular that the number of Internet users has jumped from 600,000 to 140 million and it is expected to grow further to 350 millions within the next three years.

In education, so much is the impact of Internet that even the textbook industry is going to witness a fundamental shift leave alone the periodical publications and the other forms of print media. Once a sizeable number of traders agree for sharing ideas electronically along with a higher percentage of students having access to personal computers, the situation will be quite different. Having textbooks available electronically at lower cost will enable cash strapped institutions to redirect money spent on printed textbooks for other needs. The faster the growth of technology the shorter is the time to apply it for proper gains.

With the increasing dependant on micro literature for research in the universities and the availability of improved technology for information handling, the traditional library practices of classification and cataloguing are proving to be less relevant. As the information needs of users even in the academic institutions are satisfied with some alternate means. The growing use of Internet by medical and engineering institutions is a clear indication of what is in store for the libraries of the future? PUBMED, a service of the National Library of Medicine provides access to over 11 millions of citations back to the mid 1960s and additional life science journals. It includes links to many similar websites providing full text articles and other related resources. The service is available free of cost.

Journals are the most pertinent sources of information for research in the universities. They are available in plenty on Internet. Moreover a large number of them is free of cost and if priced they cost less compared to their print counterpart. After the print media, journals could not figure in any other format except the digital media. The audiovisuals remained short lived and barring a few political ones no worth mentioning journal could surface in the audiovisual media.

Internet has also democratized the process of higher education in the true sense librating it from the clutches of the few knowledgeable and powerful without whom research was a distant dream for the students. It has affected almost every sphere of human activities. In the field of education, the work of traditional gurus has been taken over by Internet now, which provides information on the latest advancements and researches taking place in the various disciplines of study. It also supports activities of collecting data, analyzing and synthesizing it. Moreover it presents the events in international perspective hence the research work is supposed to be unique whereas the chances for repetition were higher in the past when things were perceived in the limited geographical scanario.

Internet has not only facilitated resources sharing across the boundaries of the countries but also it has freed libraries from many complicated and inconvenient practices such as the inter library lending where the documents were required to be dispatched physically. It involved risk of loss. Only the trusted institutions could render the service on the basis of mutual understanding. The idea was always good but it could never work satisfactorily.

Internet services are easily available and affordable as the cost of connectivity, computer hardware and software has come down considerably during the last few years. Moreover, there has been standardization in the ever-changing configuration of systems. The software has been made more user-friendly for computer as well as netsurfing. Now, the services are also being offered through cable TV and in case this facility widens there will be no need to purchase the computer hardware and software.

With the advent of online databases and internet, it was thought that the information technology has achieved its limits but the further advancements in cybermedia led to many other speculations and expectations for the mankind in future.

Cybermedia can be characterized as a merger or hybrid of the library, the newspaper and television, implemented on a small computer. The online database, by comparison, is a limited, specialized library with a very versatile automated card catalog. Like all specialized products, the online database assumes a certain expertise of its users.

The word cybermedia was first used in 1948 to encompass a broad range of communications between humans, between humans and machines, and between machines themselves. Within the scope of cybernetics is included the transmission of messages, especially those that exert control; the likelihood of information to degrade as time and distance intervene; and especially the function of feedback between humans and all the systems with which they have.

The ancestry of cybermedia begins with Wiener, who said, "To live effectively is to live with adequate information."McLuhan (1964) separated "cool" media, which demand active participation and an "involvement in process" from "hot" media, like print, which come in complete packages and encourage passive consumption. In McLuhan's view, roads and vehicles, money, and weapons are media, just as movies, books, and radio are. Media act as extensions of the human body, and electric media are extensions of the human nervous system.

Online databases are specialized in subject area and are often designed to serve the needs of a single academic discipline or industry group. They are expensive to create and to maintain, and gaining access to their content is also expensive, discouraging frequent and heavy usage. They presuppose knowledge of complex commands and are structured so that after the desired information has been located, the person who receives it must treat that information almost exactly like printed media (Pfaffenberger, 1990).

Cybermedia will offer a vast collection of information, stored in electronic form, that will encompass a wide variety of subject areas with a range of difficulty levels in each, encouraging schoolchildren and specialists alike to use it.Production will continue to be expensive, but so is production of television programs; a mass audience will make access to cybermedia at least as cheap as a local telephone call.

* Command structures will be self-explanatory and simple.Most important, cybermedia will break with the print tradition of finite packaged texts;It will include sound and images, both still and moving, as well as printed text.
* It will enable the people using it to compare multiple sources side-by-side, linking excerpts from numerous texts and moving among them as easily as television viewers skip among channels.
* A unilinear progression from beginning to end within a single source will be the exception instead of the rule.
* Each person will move through an open field full of pieces of data in the way that best meets his or her immediate individual needs.

4

Technology and Media in Education

Technology is defined as " a science and techniques of methods of doing or getting things done, related to an art, science or a particular profession." Technology has also been defined as the science of "industrial arts" and it is also defined as the application of science to the needs of an individual and society. Technology is a scientific way of developing new techniques, and a systematic way of evolving and applying these techniques.

Technology is thus a method of designing techniques. Information technology is a collection of technology based on computer and telecommunication and the technology employed in education is popularly known as Educational Technology, which may be defined as "an application of scientific knowledge about learning and the conditions of learning to improve the effectiveness and efficiency of teaching and training, John Leedham (1973) offered a definition of the term "educational technology" by giving a special consideration to the adopted role of the teacher". According to him, "educational technology concerns the systematic use of modem methods and technologies in teaching and learning. It involves teachers in.a variety of roles-some of which are traditional, some still emerging."

Media is the channel used for the transmission of a message as in the distinction between print sound and vision. The channels are printed messages, visually on a paper or on a screen *which* can be writing, graphics or photographs: still pictures which are transparent for projection or previewing: sound discs, moving pictures as in a live television broadcast or recorded on a cine film or videotape.

The term educational has been used in the recent times in place of 'instructional' to signify services to both teachers and students for teaching and learning. The Instructional Material Centre (IMC) and the Educational Media Centre (EMC) are conceptually parallel. Both develop from efforts to merge audiovisual services to individual students. The IMC came first initially called the audiovisual department or center. It was supposed to support group instructions with different kinds of media and its basic function was to furnish materials to faculty for teaching groups of students. As materials and equipment were developed for individual use, the later service came into being and IMC became the EMC.

A learning center is based on the concept that the library is a place where learning occurs rather than one in which learning materials are stored, its function is to promote learning by making both materials and services available to the students. Stress is laid on moving of information to the students and not on the collection of information. The role of a media librarian changes from just managing the collection to become an active member in the process of teaching and learning.

As per the American Library Association's, Standard for the school media programmes, "the terminology used to identify educational media remains in a state of change. In some Quarters, audiovisual has been replaced by media as the standard referent for those communication and learning materials which have aural and visual characteristics whether verbal or non verbal. In other quarters the expression instructional technology is being used. Recently the term media has been used to denote all modes of communication including print and audiovisual forms.

It can be observed that educational technology has three important components:

a. Defining of educational goals in specific clear terms:

b. Designing of instructional: strategies and learning sequences: and

c. Evaluation of outcomes so as to obtain indicators of success or worthlessness of educational strategies.

The process of educational technology can be defined in the following components:

a. Different students learn in different ways, and at different rates:

b. Different kinds of skills- abilities, knowledge and understandings are required in different ways:

c. The various elements of instruction themselves have different learning characteristics:

d. The elements in learning process should not be considered apart from each other as each has some bearing on education:

e. As far as possible any learning system should be self-correcting which means it should have some built-in arrangement and evaluation and feedback, which can be used to improve it.

The educational media can be defined as various media components, which are used for the purpose of education. A clear distinction and generally accepted definition has not been developed as yet though efforts have been made to define the same in own style.

The educational mass media has its practical origin from radio before World War II. British Broadcasting Company was the first to broadcast programmes for schools in 1924. They were aimed at supporting the classroom teacher. As radio is having the capability of reaching large audience simultaneously with ease and not much cost. Japan introduced school broadcasting in 1931, which was followed by Australia and New Zealand in 1932.

In India school broadcasting first started in 1938 followed by Tanzania in 1954 and Kenya in 1963. The first radio programmes were broadcast successfully in England in 1920. School broadcasting as a part of educational broadcasting began in 1924. At present, there is a huge network of local stations operating in almost all the countries of the world.

Highly developed societies concentrate on the mechanical use of audiovisual materials. Although in the less developed countries. A/V does play an important part in educational programmes. In the Government library scheme in South Italy-television is used to reach the widest audiences. India's employment based literacy programme uses audiovisual as much as possible. In such countries where there is a library service, it has an important role to play in backing up the new found literacy.

The library as a dynamic system of information storage played an important role in educational organizations. Various kinds of media got integrated through information and documentation techniques. There have been several efforts to format and standardize the descriptive catalogue of media materials. The audiovisual standards to an extent are reflected m the National Information Centre for Educational Media (NICEM), Bibliographies are available in book form. The printed catalogues are available since 1901 in the Library of Congress. The structure of all MARC formats for various media are identical but the content descriptors can be varied to extract the homomorphic transformation of different kinds of representation, film and strips, videotapes, pictures, transparencies, slides. Audiotapes, music, phonorecords, maps, serials, books etc.

The history of educational media is essentially linked with the development of new media and its application in education. Hare cited the gradual development of new media over the period since 185 with first a photograph then the phonograph followed by the silent film, the radio, the talkies and subsequent television. The demonstration electronic media in March 1970 was a landmark.

It enabled an individual to watch television programmes of ones own choice and that too at the time and place of the preference. The active participation of Europe's publishing houses at the end of the 1960 in discussions with television, videocassettes and videodiscs, these publishers formed audiovisual divisions and companies.

The term educational media was almost unknown to India till early sixties. It was used a synonym to audiovisual aids in the academic circles The advent of teaching machines, radio, television, tape recorder, computer and Internet provided a new dimension to the role of audiovisuals. The Department of Teaching Aids was established in New Delhi in 1940's which later merged with the Centre of Educational Technology (Established in 1973) to form the Central Institute of Educational Technology (CIET) ion the National Council of Educational Research and Training in 1984.

The year 1984 has great significance in the history of educational media in India since three pioneer organizations like INSAT/TV Project (lately transformed to Countrywide Classroom of the University-Grants Commission} and the Indira Gandhi National Open University (IGNOU) at New Delhi came into existence. The effective utilization of radio and educational television programmes started since then. As these organizations grew the materials produced by them in the form of audio and video films as well gathered for academic support from other agencies were also collected. These collections formed their libraries. In the year 1986, a workshop was organized by CIET on Documentation Systems for Educational Media in which the experts involved in the related field as well as some experts from Unesco participated.

Initially, the Mass Communication Research Centre at Jamia Millia Islamia developed computer software for management of media collection specially for stock shots. A private agency was involved for development of the package but the same could not work satisfactorily. With its limited resources, the Centre could not make much headway and the simple package in dBase III was developed in 1987 by the computer person and the media librarian associated with the Centre. Three separate modules *were* incorporated in the software. The most popular and utilized among them was the model meant for retrieval of information regarding the video collection. Provision of key word search was incorporated in the software to facilitate the retrieval of information.

The second major contribution in defining the role of educational media and designing the information system for them came from the Development and Educational Communication Unit (DECU) of the Indian Space Research Organization (ISRO). Ahmedabad. Being in a transmission mode and having to manage a large quantity of educational software DECU developed a computer package in collaboration of some other media organizations, computer and library professionals. Later, this package was named as VILCIX It is in active use at the Consortium for Educational Communication (CEC) New Delhi.

Along with social change has come the technological change. Society is rapidly evolving from the industrial, machine age of the electronic era. There is a continuing logarithmic increase in the use of automation in just about every human activity. It is as astounding to ponder that in less than three quarters of the last century, man was able to proceed from the first heavier-than-air flight to walking on the moon not as dramatic, put perhaps more important, is the progress in medicine and healthcare. Many of the killer epidemics that plagued man in the past are today virtually nonexistence, in achievement not with out price that world, for the first time, is faced with the critical problem of global over population, which generates a whole new set of survival problems. We are now witnessing the emergence of genetic control and manipulation and of biochemical regulation of the brain and intellect

The vast storehouses of information can now be handled electronically, but someone is to be responsible for its management.

The librarian is the obvious choice for this task, and the responsibility and power inherent in their responsibility are awesome. In a management capacity, the librarian will have considerable influence on what kind of information is selected.

The very purpose of educational technology is to facilitate and improve the quality of human learning. In order to solve the various problems of education, technology consisting of various media of mass communication and modem testing and evaluation techniques are essential. Specially, in developing countries like India, it has to be mastered and utilized by the educational administrators if they have to keep pace with each other and catch up with the developed nations.

Educational technology is concerned with providing appropriately designed learning situations which hold in view the objective of learning and the purpose of educational technology is to improve the quality of human learning. The uniqueness of educational technology is characterized as:

(i) Use of broad range of resources of learning:

(ii) Emphasis on individual learning, and

(iii) Use of systems approach.

The effectiveness of educational technology depends on:

(i) Ability to achieve goals:

(ii) To maintain itself internally; and

(iii) To adapt to its environment

The following are the reasons for application of media in education:

(a) Print media is easy to carry and it can be used according to the convenience of students. Newspapers are specifically useful for maintaining contact between scattered people.

(b) In the broadcast media, radio has enormous potential. It can cover very large audience and can reach isolated spots. Radio is within the reach of masses and should be used as a home-based means of imparting education. It supports to correspondence students by way of classroom materials and information services of various kinds

(c) TV makes it possible to use broadcasting for visual presentation. TV broadcasting is an important component in the distance education and gives the individual strength in encouraging representations by individual learners. Recently, a channel of Doordarshan has been dedicated for imparting instructión to the distant learners.

(d) Audio and video cassettes are the media which would be crucial for distance education

(e) Through the teleconferencing, the counseling sessions are arranged for students to bring the factor of two way interaction

(f) Telephone teaching can provide two way interaction between learners and teachers

(g) Video disks can be linked to the computers and the learners can interact with the materials at their own place and choice.

(h) The most convenient means at least in principle of getting textual information to member institutions is by fax. Since this arrives the same Dave in which the message is sent.

A variety of subjects of high quality make the involvement of media a must for education.

Multimedia like audio, videocassettes, telephone teaching, radio broadcast, computer learning material etc. are used at home or at the educational institutions in various parts of the country to have a face to face contact with educators to clear doubts. All theses media are educationally sound and reach to the masses at a greater extent.

The report on President's Commission on Instructional Technology has great significance with regard to the assessment of impact of technology on education. It represents the largest and the most comprehensive study ever undertaken on the relationship of man, media and machines as well as the process of educational technology. The report provides a strong foundation not only for the continued education of educators in media utilization but more significantly for the public education of all citizens. Radio, television and graphic press can be employed in the process of communicating to the general public and the possibilities for improved education. Briggs has identified the significant contribution of the report, which can be taken as characteristic problems and trends in the current status of educational media and technology;

(a) Why should not continue to bolster outdated curricula by use of new media

(b) A system model for the design of instruction should govern media decisions with specific kinds of learners in mind.

(c) The new media can help bridge the gap between school and the real world.

The information has been available in various forms of document and these forms kept changing with technologies available with time. As a result of advancement in knowledge and information, newer type of information media emerged and suitable methods need to be designed to organize their collections. A major breakthrough in this direction in the history was the invention of printing press but the invention of computer has broken all records of generation and distribution of information. The educational media with the help of telecommunication links can reach the unreached and is proving to be the most effective device in the education and learning process.

With the advancement in science and technology peoples perception of library has changed. Now, a library is regarded as more than a repository of knowledge and information. Libraries are viewed as dynamic institutions for collection and dissemination of information in whatever form or medium it is available. The educational institutions are given due consideration to the production and distribution of information contained in the non-print media.

The area includes graphics, photography and film production, audio and videotape recording and reproduction or any combination of the above said media.

The sphere of educational media is so wide that it is not possible for a researcher to carry out a comprehensive study since the varied nature of media products and services offer a range as well inconvenience in it

Possibly, the greatest change that will occur is presently on the horizon of information science. It is conceivable that in the near future libraries will he interconnected with a vast electronic information network. Electronic devices will have direct and immediate access to information stored in regional, national and international centres. This information will be retrievable and transmittable directly to the patron, home or place of employment.

The patron's access to the entire world's storehouse of information will be attained via the local libraries. Libraries will be responsible for analyzing request for information and having the expertise to interpret them by using a man-machine interface system as a means of retrieving the exact information needed. This task cannot be performed by thc unskilled patron because it requires knowledge in the operation and efficient use of information systems.

Retrieving electronically stored information will be only part of the library profession's task. It will also include determining what data are to be entered into the information bank, to what media format the data are to be committed, and what information is to be rejected or discarded. The system will include a feedback poon with a two-way flow of information between the smallest library and the largest information bank. Obviously such a system will involve a highly sophisticated electronic network managed by a capably trained professional.

It is difficult to comprehend the impact electronic technology is having and will continue to have on the libraries. The library could become the manager of all mankind's recorded information worthy of being preserved, with the ability to make this information directly accessible on demand to any patron anywhere. The librarian will need to be acquainted with the procedures involved in materials selection, to develop efficient system approaches to implanting the procedures, to be aware of how information can be distributed.

Nolan has listed the following needs and challenges in view of the technological developments:

(1) Increased training in the use of audiovisual materials, but far more important will be the need for imagination, initiative and special planning.

(2) More intensive need for studies of needs for audiovisual materials: their usefulness, effectiveness and relationship to the requirements of teaching and library services.

(3) Expansion of technological research and automation to permit a greater degree of use through self service and through mass service.

(4) Greater coordination of the various audiovisual forms with one another and with print materials through more intensive programming.

(5) Development of more bibliographic coverage and methods of organization of audiovisual materials for use.

Librarians ignoring the systems needs have developed audiovisual services using the methods of print oriented organization of resources and their cataloguing. Grieco consequently exhorts librarians to provide the same intellectual accessibility for non-print materials that is now accorded to print.

The advent of teaching machines i.e. radio, television- tape record, computer and language laboratory provided a new dimension to the role of audiovisual aids. Technology in education lays stress on the concept of service like technology in the service of farming or agriculture or science in the service of mankind. It is concerned with the use of technical advancements in terms of various equipments materials and machines for educational purposes. It is involving audiovisual equipment, hardware and sophisticated electronic devices such as radio, television, film, projectors, tape recorders etc.

There are two technologies, which have contributed emerging educational media viz, video and computer. There are of course varieties of modes in which these two are presented as different instructional media.

Video in Education includes the following components :

(a) Videocassettes with VCR/VCP and Television

(b) Broadcasting video programmes, live or recorded and distributed through microwave stations to satellite coupled with direct receiving sets (DRS) or relay stations e.g. SITE and UGC's Countrywide Classroom or school telecast of CIET

(c) Closed Circuit Television

(d) Able TV

(e) Community Antenna

(i) Interactive Television

(g) Telex, and

(h) Videtex

Computer technology offers the following in the field of education:

(a) Computer Managed Instruction

(b) Computer Assisted Instruction

(c) Computer Based Education

(d) Intelligent CAI

(e) Artificial Intelligence

(f) CAD/CAM

(g) Expert Systems

(h) Microprocessor Based Educational Kit for Laboratories and Workshops

A combination of varieties of motionpictures, slides, computer data, text, music, speech etc. are using computer and laser technology.

These technologies are particularly relevant for distance education because of the inherent simplicity of audio as a communication medium, its capacity to invoke the imagination of listener, promote his/her active participation in the learning process, its easy reach economy etc. The audio formats usually employed in education are:

(a) Talk by eminent experts

(b) Discussions regarding controversial/complex problems

(c) Question answer series containing frequently asked questions (FAQ) on a given subject

(d) Audio updates as quick revisions for the printed lessons

(e) Language learning

(f) Features/drama on historical topics

Universities have also started producing 'blind friendly' lessons. These are audio transformations of the print materials so that the audio is self sufficient in itself for the independent use of visually impaired. Such audio transformations are also found useful for the course in which the literacy level of the target group is generally very low.

Alongside the non-broadcast use of audio in the form of taped lessons, radio broadcasting is equally popular means of serving the need of education. The reach of radio now extends to all nooks and corners of the world.

While radio broadcasts are useful in their own way. the fact of broadcasting is a one-way medium limits their use in the educational context. Phnoe-in-programme through radio can overcome this limitation to a large extent. Once radio counseling takes root, it can be used as an alternative to face to face counseling.

Video, television and other audiovisual media have obvious application for education because of their ability to carry both visual and oral messages to recreate a classroom atmosphere for the learners. Even though much costlier than audio-based media, they are pedagogically very effective and in fact unavoidable whenever the subject matter involves visual portrayal of real events, explanation through graphic animation etc.

Videotapes deal with topics/concepts requiring visual exposition that cannot be adequately dealt through print or audio media. They are also used to record renowned authorities and scientists in their respective areas of specialization, to serve as reference material for the students. Production formats for video vary depending upon the subject matter and target groups involved. In the simplest case, their video lectures containing the teacher's image and voice, the occasional visual inserts relevant to the topic. On the other hand, documentaries, which portray real life situation, on location-visuals and dramatized portrayal recreating a particular historical period are also produced.

Videos for natural sciences are helpful for demonstration of science practical, magnifying view of microscopic objects, graphical explanation of process, reactions etc.

Educational videos produced for different courses through the various production agencies like IGNOU, EMRCs/AVRCs/ MCRC/CIET etc. are trimmed and capsuled to suit the telecast mode of the television. IGNOU's video programmes are telecast daily through the primary channel of Doordarshan.

Interactivity is the foremost requirement for video-based technologies as in the case of audio-based technologies. This consideration has prompted to start the Training and Development Communication Channel with the help of Indian Space Research Organization (ISRO). This is one way video/two way audio teleconferencing system, with the teaching end of the EMPC studios and learning ends located at all the regional centres.

Computer can do all the things to facilitate qualitative learning. Software techniques programmes are stored and transmitted through input devices including computer-based training. The objective of using computer based media in distance education as suggested by J. Rama Naidu are:

(1) To make distance education more effective

(2) To strengthen and sustain interest in learning

(3) To cater to individual differences in learning preferences and abilities.

(4) To provide feedback

(5) To help the learners solve their problems easily.

(6) To improve the standards of distance education.

(7) To inspire or initiate teachers to change their method of teaching by exploring different possibilities

(8) To bridge the distance between the teacher and the student.

In recent years, penetration of computers and computer networks even in the developing countries has been phenomenal. Even though individual ownership of computers in the country is negligible, their instructional availability and usage is well neigh universal with even small size establishments generally using one. In the beginning use of computers was restricted to scientific and administrative functions but of late it was extended to the library services. Their use as a "surrogate teacher' and as a medium in the mainstream of the multimedia academic packages has started more recently.

Some institutions have started producing and distributing courseware on CD ROMs. IGNOU produces entire duration course on CD ROMs for BCA and MCA programmes so that students may use them as and when needed as an alternative to the printed text. Apart from the huge storage capacity (One CD ROM can contain the material of whole programme) they can be used in an interactive way enabling the *power* points sides and streaming audio and video which can provide a model of just in time or on demand multimedia lectures. CD ROMs produced by IGNOU are used by students in the standalone modes since computer students are expected to have better understanding and involvement with the latest technologies.

Multimedia is not a machine or system or a newly discovered principle. It is defined multimedia as an objective describing a multi sensory approach to the disbursement and acquisition of information: text and pictures, still graphics and motion video. Pictures and text manipulated with buttons and slide bars.

A videodisc is similar to CD that holds still images, video segments and sounds. The advantages of video disc over video tape or videocassette is its high quality of images- still frames, fast access to any part of disc, freedom from wear and expansive mass production. When combined with computer, videodisc becomes a powerful audiovisual database for interactive teaching and learning. Information on disk cannot be changed by the user. Disadvantage is the playback only and its high production cost.

The constant linear velocity (CLV) is primarily used for linear playback application such as movies, musical performance and so on. These discs may be recorded with one frame per track near the centre of the disc and up to three frames per track near the outside of the disc. Due to this quality, CLV videodisc must be played at the speed varying from 1800/rpm (revolution per minute) near the centre to 600/rmp near the outside. Thus it plays at a speed of 30 frames per second- required to be compatible with National Standard Television Committee (NTSC) video, and therefore, displayable on standard television sets. The CLV videodisc permits a forward and reverse scanning as dual channel audio and chapter stops. But CLV is relatively limited in its interactive potential.

Microcomputers are often considered to fall within the domain of libraries because they are similar to other machines and software systems already located there and it is presumed that the audiovisual library professional is more likely comparing with others to know and administer them. In most types of libraries, microcomputers can be found in a variety of other places as well such as departments as systems, cataloguing, children and public service often find themselves.

Internet is being used by academic institutions as a delivery system for the courses. Despite the constraint of poor individual computers and Internet connectivity. It is being recently used for the following purposes:

(a) Downloading/browsing rapidly changing information such as schedules and announcements, assignment or even short samples of course materials.

(b) E-mail for operational and academic support- and communication with fellow students.

(c) Using FAQs to answer the queries: both academic and otherwise

(d) Using chat to interact with teachers and fellow students

After the invention of the printing press and computer. Internet is the next paradigm shift in human life. It has provided a powerful medium of communication for individuals of different tastes. And education is no exception. Virtual universities are being established all over the world and the beginning has already been made in India with about all major cities organizing such institutional support to the students. One can enroll with such universities for the desired academic course without being physically present.

With increasing convergence between computer and communication technologies and the spread of telecommunication networks, present day open universities are expected to gradually transform themselves as virtual universities where all functions of the university will take place electronically over the digital links and networks,

During the last two decades, the importance of non-book materials as carriers of information has got a wider recognition along with the technical aids to retrieve information from them. Librarians have accepted that just as they have responsibility for facilitating retrieval of information from books, they also have equal responsibility for the newer types of materials

5

Growth of Educational Media

Education has always been the basic need of mankind. It comes through, instructions based on materials and methods. Information is the prime resource for instruction whether imparted verbally or through some other ways and the degree of utility of information largely depends upon the way of its presentation and also the perception process of human beings.

The terminology defined to identify educational media remains in the state of change. In some quarters, audiovisual has been replaced by media as the standard reference for communication and learning materials, which has aural and visual characteristics whether verbal or non verbal. In other quarters, the expression instructional technology is being used. However, a generally accepted definition of educational media refers to all modes of communication including print and audiovisual forms, which are used for educational and instructional purposes.

The electronic media now accommodates all types of media whether text, audio or video or a combination of them and provide tremendous help for disseminating the information. Its sensitively produced message transmitted in different forms is received universally and by and large is understandable even by those who are not literate or are residing in the remote area of the world having a variety of cultural contacts and possessing marginal visual literacy.

In India, the success of satellite based broadcasting television programmes is already well established. The country is now one of the few nations who have made rapid strides in modernizing communication system and techniques. The Government of India has also taken keen interest in satellite delivery system for television with specific understanding that it is used for education.

The Oxford English Dictionary (1989) defines education as "the process of nourishment or rearing a child or young person, an animal" whereas according to the Columbia Encyclopedia, education" includes any process shaping the potentialities of maturing organism and may be formal or informal. Informal education results form the constant effect of the environments and its strength in shaping the values and habits can hardly be over estimated. Formal education is a conscious effort by society to impart the skills and the needs of thought considered essential (Columbia Encyclopedia, 1950). The Encyclopedic Dictionary of the World defines education as systematic instruction given by each succeeding generation to the young of the race to fit them for the work of the life (Encyclopedia Dictionary of the world, 1989)

Media refers to the various means of mass communication thought of as a whole, including television, radio, magazines and newspapers, together with the people involved in their production. Marshall McLuhan (1962) categorizes media into two opposing poles; hot and cold: hot media, a medium that intends one single sense in high definition to a state of being well filled with data like a radio and cool media, 'a medium of definition demanding a high level of completion by the audience'. One of the most popular search engine available on the Internet, i.e. yahoo.com contains 267 web pages on "educational media" which include all type of technical materials and aids being provided in education.

The ALA Glossary of Library and Information sciences (1983) published by the American Library Association defines the term educational media as audiovisual materials, which have been designed and produced for instructional purpose.

The keystone in education is communication, a give and take of ideas, which blend into a mutual understanding of theory, principle and facts. If education is to fulfill its primary mission, that of transmitting the cultural heritage from generation to generation and assisting youths in growing to their adult role more emphasis must be placed upon the understanding of the communication process and more attention devoted to the improvement of effective communication techniques.

It is popularly believed that educational media is something new, which was introduced with the discovery of electricity. But it is not so because during the primitive age, man roamed sections of the earth, many forms of communication were used and developed. As Brooker (1949) observes, "he grunted his way to phonetic speech, figured and doubled his way to art, used his muscles to develop the many forms of dance, and learned to give meaning by the pitch of his voice, and the way he used the muscles of his face. He gathered pieces of stick and lay them in his track blazed trees to tell others of the path, used the smoke of his campfire to carry his messages, used his hands to talk with strangers, developed rituals to tell the story of his tribes."

The impact of media as emerged out of the technical innovations in new formats like photographs, audio, video multimedia and Internet shapes the styles of thinking and though whether in the area sociology, arts, science or religion. Alvin Toffler in his book 'The third wave' defines this phenomenon and terms information technology as the ultimate technology.

New media is advantageous for the educational institutions in many ways. The printed publications now cost more comparing with their digital counterparts. Basically, there are two main factors responsible for escalation in the price of printed publications—the revision of prices, and the ever-eroding conversion value of the Indian currency in the international market. Even the mass production does not help. Quoted below are examples illustrating the hike in case of a periodical publication, an encyclopedia and a book. All the publications have been produced on mass scale.

Looking at the pricing pattern of the printed publications, it is found that the publishers increase the price after one or two years. On the contrary, cost of the electronic media is decreasing fast. The *Encyclopacdia Britannica* is available on multimedia disc and CD-ROM much cheaper than its print counterpart. Multimedia can be termed as quite a different form because of its way of presentation but the same information is available on CD-ROM as on paper. It is important to clarify here that the expenditure on hardware is now within the affordable limits. Actually the expenditure on CD-RUM disc drive is made once and that too not exclusively for the *Encyclopedia Britannica* but also for many other sources. Now, titles are emerging directly in the form of electronic media and in the times to come, their quantum is expected to be so high that even the rate of generation of information in print will be affected.

The expenses being incurred on books and journals can conveniently be reduced to half in case the potential of Internet is utilized properly. It is a good substitute to a huge number of reference tools, journals and books. Moreover, the updated information is instantly available on it all the time. Like in the area of medicine, efforts on international level are on to serve humanity in the field of education. New web sites are being launched on Internet day by day for education of the masses. They may be visited on will with out any barrier and the information contained in them can be downloaded for future use.

In the field of library and information profession which is concerned with the storage and dissemination of information in all its manifestations including the latest media, the modernization and automation efforts in the beginning were aimed at reducing the repetitive processes by introducing one time entry of data provision, in order to improve the efficiency and effectiveness in service. Prior to the 1970, it was the application of punched card based system using mechanical card sorting and tabulating equipment manufactured largely by IBM Corporation. With the beginning of 1980's it was evident that computer and communication technology were making possible a number of trends in library and information services. Libraries witnessed a major change in the nature of documents that they were supposed to accommodate as substitute to manuscripts and printed books, which already became their traditional and natural repositories. Now, they accommodate all types of' information products including audiovisuals in their various forms ranging, from celluloid to software of computers.

The task of learning the various media categories is quite simple, and indeed most people are familiar with most of them as an integral part of their everyday lives. The categories are not finite or closed, and it is possible that some information forms could be assigned to more than one category, but again, knowing the various categories, one should know what a particular medium does and how it can be used. Classifying material as print or non-print is ambiguous and not very helpful, print information can be found in many media (e.g. paper, microform, computer, videodisc). Mediated, as opposed to non mediated, indicates only whether or not it is necessary to nave some device or piece of equipment to information. For instance, a book does not require any device, whereas a film required a piece of projection equipment. But, with the proliferation of information available today, it could well be that some information items are available in both mediated and no mediated forms (Booker, 1949)

Educational media contain a larger body of information in a condensed form. If a researcher gathers 100% of available information on his subject then only 10% of the information is used for effective presentation to exploit the various sense organs of man, whether in the script itself or the commentary spoken or visual presentation of facts. Yet the script writer needs to be in command of the other 90% of information, to back him up with the necessary endorsement confirmation in support which he in order to be able to state with confidence that his information is complete and accurate. In the words of Prof. James A. Beverage (1975), a renowned documentary filmmaker and a UNESCO expert on educational media "the visible information in a film, the information contained expressed in the story and stated in the dialogue and commentary resemble the proportion of an iceberg which can be seen floating on the surface of the ocean. Only one eighth of the iceberg can be seen on the surface of the water- seven eighths of its bulk is below the surface and cannot be seen. This gives an analogy with the information contained of a film (Beverage, 1975). Only a small proportion of the facts are literary seen or heard in such a presentation". It means that whatever is not seen or heard at one time or to an individual may be understood in different situations.

Media perform four basic functions (Hicks and Tillin, 1997) i.e. Informational functions, Cultural functions, and Recreational functions. Its Educational functions are as below :

* To provide for continuous life long education
* To create and sustain broad academic interest, creativity and intellectual activity, and to support intellectual freedom
* To encourage perceptual sensitivity and occupational competence
* To promote positive social attitude and a democratic society.

These functions further serve the whole of society, including all ethnic, educational economic, and social strata within society.

Technology has brought crucial change in the pattern of generating and acquiring knowledge. Earlier, it was the technology of audiovisual aids that developed at a very high speed. Now, the rapid emergence of computers, multimedia, CD ROM materials as in its way defined the change from analog to digital systems and along with the change has come with increasingly pervasive emphasis on computer based technologies and multimedia. design and access. Moreover, digital network technology that is the Internet, digital satellite system etc. and the soon to be universal High Definition

Television (HDTV) has further radicalized the information field. The following are the responsible for steady growth of educational media in India:

Radio and television have been the traditional carriers of educational media to the masses so far. They serve the learners of all levels through input from various programme production agencies. The network of television expanded very fast to cover various regions if the country so that the programmes in different language could be produced and telecast. Recording and reproduction facilities in media made it possible for an individual to decide which media programme to watch, with whom to watch and when to watch. The only disadvantage of smaller size of screen of television and computer was that it is not suitable for larger gatherings like a classroom situation but this is also a fact that due to increased specialization in education the size of class is being reduced day by day. On the other hand the advancement of scientists have invented device to enlarge the screen so as to make it possible for the larger groups to watch in large gatherings. Computer is also being used in education in the advanced countries as it can stores large amount of information and display it as and when needed. In India, some educational institutions have already introduced computer for the educational and instructional purposes.

UGCs INSAT'/TV Project popularly known as the Countrywide Classroom was launched at the Mass Communication Research Centre, Jamia Millia Islamia, New Delhi. It heralded an era for the educational communication in the country. A number of Educational Media Research Centres/Audio Visual Research Centres were established to augment the process of production of educational software.

In 1984 only 20% indigenous programmes were telecast on Doordarshan whereas by 1992 this ratio was just reversed and 80% of the productions were produced within the country. Now a separate TV channel of educational communication is working in the country like the other advanced nations and the ratio of indigenously produces educational software is very high comparing with the last decade.

The University Grants Commission appointed a Curriculum Development Committee to design common curricula for all the universities. It was a positive sign for the media production agencies. Earlier they had problem in deciding the contents of a programme since the syllabi of nearly all the institutions were different. Now, producers are. able to identify the themes of the programmes that have the widest application.

A number of educational media production agencies have been established for production of hardware. These agencies include, Doordarshan, Inter University Consortium for Educational Communication; lass Communication Research Centre/Educational Media Centres/Audio Visual Research Centre i, Central Institute of Educational Technology/State Institutes of Educational Technology/District Institute of Educational Technology, Indian Institutes of Technology, Technical Teachers Training Institutes, Agriculture Universities, Indira Gandhi National Open University/ Electronic' Media Production Centre, Central Institute of Indian languages and other Govt. and private; agencies.

From the decade of 1980's onwards, a number of educational media organizations have come into existence. They include government as well as private agencies. Some of the popular media organizations are the following:

(a) **Central Institute of Educational Technology (CIET). New Delhi :** CIET at the National Council of Educational Research and Training, New Delhi is a premier media organization of the country, mainly entrusted with the work of producing educational software for radio and television programmes. It is involved in the teaching and learning enhancement of the schoolteachers and students through its various activities.

The beginning of the CIET Library can be stated in 1942 as an adjunct to the Department of Education of the Government of India. After independence it formed the nucleus of the Audio Visual

Section of the Ministry of Education in 1948. With the birth of National Institute of Audio Visual Education in 1959, it became a part of the Institute. In 1961, when the Institute was merged with NCERT, it was renamed as the Department of Teaching Aids and the Central Film Library became as one of its major sections.

Central Film Library has a collection of about 5000 films with about 8.500 prints. Out of these about 300 titles are in color. The Library has about 20 feature films also and a number of documentaries of the Film Division. Apart from the educational film and videos- the Library holds a sizeable collection of audiotapes also.

The Library follows standardized techniques of classification and cataloguing and provides subject heading to its holdings. But it has no computer hardware and software. It experiences lack of staff. There are only two persons available in the Library whereas with the audiovisual media it also houses collection of print media.

CIET organizes workshops and training programmes for the staff of SIETs and DIETs in management of library collections and documentation. One such seminar was organized in collaboration with UNESCO in 1986 and its theme was Documentation Systems for Educational Media. Later on in 1992, another workshop was organized on management of media collections in CIET. SIET and DIET libraries

(b) **Consortium for Educational Communication, New Delhi:** Consortium for Educational Communication (CEC) was established in 1993 to undertake the challenging activities relating top the Countrywide Classroom of the University Grants Commission (1) CEC has the responsibility for 'coordination with the media centers- the University Grants Commission and television as well as for overall system management related to the broadcast of educational programmes.

CEC is the custodian of all the master tapes produced by the

Media Centers and has a computerized Media Tape Library with up-to-date storage and retrieval facilities. It also has facilities for programme production and dobbing of English programmes in other Indian languages through a digital audio workstation.

The Library of CEC is equipped with the latest gadgets as needed for preview of the audiovisual media. It houses about 6,000 video programmes on tapes in U Matte and Betacam formats. The collection of the Library is enriched from the Educational Media Research Centres (EMCs) and Audio Visual Media Research Centres (AVRCs) which are spread through out the country and are entrusted with the work of producing educational software for the university level students. CEC Library follows standardized norms for processing the collection of audiovisual media. It has introduced DDC for classification and AACRI for cataloguing and subject headings are assigned through the Library of Congress List of Subject Headings. The media collection is shelved in chronological order according to the media centres.

E-mail and Internet facilities have been provided to the Library. For which sufficient computer hardware support is available. One of the most significant feature is that the Library uses a software for its operations which has specifically been designed for the tape libraries with assistance from the Development and Educational Communication Unit of the Space Application Centre, Ahmedabad.

Apart form providing the normal library service, CEC organized Workshops on Documentation of Media Libraries and train staff engaged in the media centres in the techniques of managing the media library collections.

The future plans of CEC Library include Networking among all the media centre libraries through out the country and cooperation among libraries for exchange and dissemination of information through e-mail and Internet facilities if available to all the media centres

(c) Electronic Media Production Centre, New Delhi : The

Electronic Media Production Centre (EMPC) is situated at the Sanchar Kendra of the Indira Gandhi National Open University (IGNOU) New Delhi. It is equipped with the state of the art technology. EMPC is the Centre from which the Gyan Darshan-Educational TV Channel of Doordarshan telecast its programmes.

EMPC produces audio an video courseware of IGNOU programmes, disseminate educational programmes through both broadcast and non-broadcast modes, coordinates with the broadcasting and distribution agencies, adapts and integrates new communication technologies for distance learning: develops quality courseware in media studies and provides hand on experimental training and educational institutions/agencies, conducts researches to strengthen the content utilization ad delivery aspects of distance learning: develops and offers audio/video library resources designs and coordinate pilot projects in the application of communication technology to improve and strengthen distance learning, undertakes marketing and sale of EMPC/IGNOU products and facilities.

The present collection of EMPC Library includes about 5.000 video and 1,000 audio programmes. The materials are arranged in the Library according to the courses being offered by IGNOU. The Library is not using any standardized method for classification and cataloguing of its holdings and no subject headings are assigned to the ,volumes.

(d) **The Commonwealth Educational Media Centre for the Asia (CEMCA)** : CEMCA was founded in 1987 by the Commonwealth Heads of Government at their meeting in Vancouur, Canada. The Commonwealth of Learning (COL) has a mandate to the development of knowledge resources and technology for learning through out Commonwealth countries. CEMCA is hosted by the Indira Gandhi National Open University in India and it covers the Asian Commonwealth region comprising of Bangladesh. Brunei,

India, Malaysia, The Maldives, Pakistan, Singapore and Sri Lanka.

(a) Media databases

CEMCA Media Database contains information about audio and video programmes developed by the educational institutions in the region. The database can be searched through title- keyword, subjects, producer, institution and many other options. The database is constantly updated and is made available off line to participating institutions twice through CD ROM services.

(b) Educational Media Links

This facility links all the educational media organizations of the Commonwealth countries such as radio, TV, online information networks etc.

(c) Archives

CEMCA operates as a regional service to COL. Workshop on multimedia courseware and development on media management are on the anvil. It also covers educational materials on application of television production techniques of teleteaching.

(d) Promotion of Research

CEMCA promotes research on use of information and communication technologies through appropriate funding, training and capacity building of researchers. Research proposals are also invited from interested scholars and researches within the scope of CEMCA's mandate through out the year of consideration. Currently, thrust areas of research at CEMCA include:

(1) Use of multimedia by distance learners

(2) Learning from multimedia

(3) Use of ICT for development and training

(4) Internet and World Wide Web

(5) ITC for people with disabilities

(6) Digital divide

(7) Gender issues in technology use in education.

(e) Indian Institute of Mass Communication Library. New Delhi

The Indian Institute of Mass Communication (IIMC) was established in 1965. The institute has been functioning as an autonomous center for advanced study in mass communication training and research and is fully funded by the Government of India through the Ministry of Information and Broadcasting.

In 1969, a major programme- the postgraduate diploma course in journalism for developing countries was started. In addition a number of courses were started to meet training need of communication professionals working in various media/publicity outfits of the central and state governments and public sector organizations. In 1981-82. the Institute started a course in broadcast journalism for in-service personnel from Akashvani and Doordarshan. The Institute has recently started a training programme in radio and television journalism.

The IIMC has the largest specialized library in mass communication in the country. It has collected about 26000 volumes of different aspects of mass communication and allied subjects such as print media, broadcasting, advertising, communication, communication research, public relations, radio and television, film, information technology and traditional media.

The periodical section of the Library subscribes to about 200 periodicals. It has documented about 20,000 articles form periodicals on different aspects of mass communication such as communication research, journal of broadcasting etc. Indian journals on mass communication such as Communicator, Vidusa, Inkword, Journal of Communication and Culture etc. are also received in the Library. Documentation Unit of the Centre has compiled bibliography on mass communication literature in four volumes, which were published in 1975. 1982. 1986 and 1989. The Library also brines out a Current Awareness Service listing articles published in books and journals.

The Library uses computer and has created database of its holdings. Presently, it uses LIBSYS software. It has purchased 84 videocassettes and has two TV and VCP sets. It is linked to DELNET.

(f) Technology Information Forecasting and Assessment Centre. New Delhi

Technology Information Forecasting and Assessment Centre (TIFAC) is an autonomous organization under the department of Science and Technology of Government of India. It was established in 1988. TIFAC (8) aims to keep technology watch on global trends and formulation preferred technology options for India. It has the following objectives:

(1) Undertake technology assessment and forecasting studies in selected area of national economy.

(2) Watch global trends and formulation of preferred options for India.

(3) Establish a nationally accessible technology information system: and

(4) Promotion of key technologies

TIFAC's Information Technology Service takes a lead role as 'technology advisor' both for Indian Industry as well as corporate companies who are keen to do business with India. It is the "single technology window' for providing an effective interface with the related R&D Labs. Experts and Companies for Technology development including aspects of human resources development like training etc. TIFAC helps industry by providing the following information services:

(a) Database on Indian Patents

Database on Indian Patents is available now with Patent Facilitating Centre from CD ROM discs. The database relates to the patent applications filed and patent applications accepted and notified for opposition. The CD ROM can be run on the Windows 95 and its advanced versions. The database are quite user friendly and equipped with latest search tools and logic operations

(b) Customized Information Service

Specialized Technology -cum- Business Opportunity Report are compiled by TIFAC. It offers technology support services in a number of scientific and technological allocations.

(c) Technology Expert Network

A roster of Indian technology experts from industry, academic and research laboratories have been maintained. The database gives an impetus to provide a common platform for experts to share their experiences globally.

Apart form the above services TIFAC offers Technology Sourcing Worldwide Database containing around 4.000 technology offers from India and abroad and to propose and offer technology in the various field of knowledge.

(g) Asian Academy of Film and Television. NOIDA, U.P.

Academy of Film and Television (AAFT) was established in 1993. It is the prime institution of its kind in private sector of India, which provides training to professionals in film and television media. Presently AAFT conducts comprehensive short term training courses aimed at creating a balance of theoretical knowledge, practical skulls and work attitude with view to fulfill the perceived need of media professionals. So far, over 2,400 persons have been trained at the AAFT. It has its own extensive studio complex, the equipment and books and video library required for conducted the training courses. The guest faculty is drawn from the eminent practicing film and television professionals to keep the trainees in touch with the real world time frame.

International Film and Television Research Center (IFTRC) at AAFT conduct research with audience on programmes and effectiveness. It stands for encouraging and popularizing the concept of mass media and train media researches to add better TV programmes and filmmaking. The aims and objectives of IFTRC are as under:

(a) Advancement of film and television production.

(b) Raising of professional standard of filmmaking and television production.

(c) Creating awareness about responsive film and television production.

(d) Continuing review of professional codes and ethics set by the professional and regulatory bodies for filmmakers and television training.

(e) Exploring the need for raining the standard of film and television training.

(f) Arranging scholarships, awards and organizing travels for purpose of research in film and television

(g) Facilitating attachment to film and television production houses for the purpose of research.

(h) Conducting short term and long-term courses on media research.

(i) Establishing databank and clearing house of information on film and television training,

(j) Publishing papers reports and books relating to research on film and television.

(k) Launching journal of media research.

AAFT's Library is at the growing stage. Presently, it holds about 1,000 videocassettes besides 150 films and 500 books. The Library collection is not classified, catalogued as no professional librarian has been employed there. The Library is having many hardware items including Telephone. Cameras, projectors and audio and video recorders and players.

(h) Indira Gandhi National Centre for the Arts Library. New Delhi.

The Indira Gandhi National Centre for the Arts (AGNCA) was launched in New Delhi in November 1985 by the Late Prime Minister Mrs. Indira Gandhi with the following aims and objectives:

(a) To evolve mode of research programmes and arts administration more pertinent to the Indian ethos

(b) To elucidate the formative and dynamic factors in the complex web of interactions between complex social strata, communities and religions.

(c) To promote national network with national and international institutions, and

(d) To conduct related research in the arts- humanities and culture.

Recognizing the need to encompass and preserve the distributed fragments of Indian art and culture, a pioneer attempt has been made by IGNCA to serve as a major resource center for arts specially, written and oral and visual materials. One of the programme of the Centre in collaboration of United Nations Development (UNDP) is to utilize multimedia computer technology to create a wide variety of software packages that communicate cultural information.

Multimedia technology allows the users to interact and explore the subject in a non-linear mode by combining audio, text, graphics animation and video on a computer.

IGNCA Library is developing a photo and slide collection of over 1 lakh objects and illustrated miniatures in Indian and foreign collections. This includes collections from Victoria and Albert Museum . Chester Betty Collection and Indian National Trust for Cultural Heritage (INTAC).

IGNCA is National Information System and Data Bank of arts humanities-cultural heritage with a fully supported reference library and multimedia collection, which serves as a major resource center. It is proposed to have a very large library of microfilm and microfiches along with the printed materials. Language is not a barrier in its collection development policy It is also proposed to have a collection of about half a million works during the next few years. The various divisions containing the media collections are as under:

(a) Reference Library

(b) Printed Materials

(c) Microfilm and Microfiches

(d) Visual Library

(e) Information and Databank

(f) Literature

(g) Architecture and Sculpture

(h) Photographs

(i) Music

(j) Film and Video

(k) Living legend Series.

The Library of IGNCA has is equipped with a range of hardware and software items including HP3000/42, Touch Screen PC. ECS/1000 Terminals. Laser Printer, Document Scanner. The Software used by the Library is MINISIS IMAGE. CDS/ISIS. LIBSYS. ROXPRO, LOTUS. VIDURA etc. Library has completed computerization in the areas of cataloguing, acquisition- serial circulation and control. The Library participated in DELNET and provides E-mail, online. Internet and CD ROM facility.

(i) Audio Visual Telecasting Unit. Parliament House. New Delhi

Audio Visual Telecasting Unit (AVTU) is the part of India's

Parliament Library which holds around a million volumes of books, reports, government publications, U.N. reports, debates, gazettes and other documents including periodicals brought out by the Lok Sabha Secretariat. AVTU is dedicated to the recording of the Parliament Proceedings and other important events.

Televising of select Parliamentary Proceedings in India commenced with the live telecast of President's Address to the Members of both the House of Parliament on the 20 of December 1989. After that there has been a regular telecasting of Question Hour. Railways and General Budget and Debates/Discussions on Motion of ''Thanks on President's Address". Demands for Grants and No Confidence Motion in the Council of Ministers.

The Unit coordinates with Doordarshan/All India Radio and other official agencies for the telecast/broadcast of Parliamentary Proceedings, National and International Conferences/Seminars besides other important Parliamentary precincts and elsewhere. It has acquired Linguaphone Courses (audio and videocassettes) in 7 Indian languages. It has also added to its collection audiocassettes pertaining to classical, instrumental music and patriotic songs for use at various parliamentary functions: these could be listened by the members in the Viewing Room. Videocassettes of Lok Sabha proceedings since 18 April 1994 and all the parliamentary events etc. are available in the Audio Visual Library holdings.

AVTU follows Universal Decimal Classification and catalogue its holding as per a local system. It arranges the audiovisual materials in a chronological order. It posses a Unix Computer and uses LibSys for management of the Library collection, A database of its holdings has already been created. The Library has been given more space for housing of the collection and will soon be shifted to its new location in the new building.

(j) Mass Communication Research Centre Library, New Delhi

Mass Communication Research Centre at the Jamia Millia

Islamia, New Delhi was established in 1982 with the cooperation of the Canadian International Development Agency and the York University of Canada to train manpower in the art of film radio and video production.

Along with the training the Centre produces film, radio and television programmes and is a regular contributor to the Countrywide Classroom of the University Grants Commission. The projects for production of media programmes are assigned to the students, which are also telecast on TV, and radio. MCRC has a well stocked Media Library with 6.500 video programmes. The Library is equipped with the traditional as well as latest gadgets to preview the productions, which are processed according to the established library techniques. The Library has also documented the rare segments contained in the video productions of the Centre with an objective to reuse such shots of films in future in order to reduce the cost of production.

Apart from the above software producing agencies a number of governmental and private institutions have also come up to contribute the field of education and training by way of educational progrmmes.

6

Development of Media Collection

Most academic libraries collect media materials, primarily audio and video formats. Media collections are as diverse and vital as any print collection in an academic library. The new media of communication is user-friendly therefore, it became easier for the common man to understand the reality. The audio visual media and multimedia which is a confluence of all types of documents, provided opportunity to perceive happenings directly in the mind unlike the print.

The task of learning the various media categories is quite simple, and indeed most people are familiar with most of them as an integral part of their everyday lives. The categories are not finite or closed, and it is possible that some information forms could be assigned to more than one category. The librarian should know what a particular medium does and how it can be used. The following categories are based primarily on the physical characteristics of the items.

Libraries are involved in a wide range of media and the librarian needs to be aware of the various media categories. No longer can it suffice for materials to be classified simply as print or non-print is mediated or non-mediated. Classifying material as print or non-print is ambiguous and not very helpful. Print information can be found in many media such as paper, microform, computer, videodisc.

Mediated, as opposed to non mediated, indicates only whether or not it is necessary to have some device or piece of equipment to information. For instance, a book does not require any device, whereas a film requires a piece of projection equipment. But. with the proliferation of information available today it could well be that some information items are available in both mediated and no mediated forms.

A book can be available in a bound copy or it can be available on microfilm. It is still a book; however in the latter form, it requires the use of a microfilm reader in order to be read. Considering whether an item is mediated assists the librarian in a search, there would obviously be no need to search for a videotape if the library does not have access to videotape playback equipment. There are many other forms in which the educational media is available in libraries and some of them are being discussed below:

The most common form of a document is a book. Most books are bound with hard covers however paperback books are becoming more prevalent. Reference books, and more specifically, encyclopedias, are generally available in hard cover. Selection aids are also available in book form, both hard cover and paperback. Books are also classified as fiction or nonfiction. A more specific classification is that of a textbook, the definition of which can be quite nebulous. Some librarians consider any book, even a novel, a textbook if it is required reading for a particular course of instruction and organizes information in a concise format by which the reader can receive instruction and learn and verify information by virtue of its accuracy and authenticity. Dissertations or research papers would be considered quasi textbooks because although they are not primarily intended to instruct, they do inform and provide scholarly information.

Community resources include things available from the community and fall into two major areas: (a) things in the community that cannot be brought to the library but must be seen on actual location and would be classified as field trip items, arid (b) things from the community that can be brought into the library and would be called local realia. A sub area or type of this category would be resource persons, people available to the library, who can make a contribution to a topic for which the librarian is preparing a bibliography.

Although it is unlikely that individual libraries will be having their own computers. There is a growing number of computer terminals available to the library patron. The computer terminal is the means by which the user can introduce, obtain, and interact with information stored in a computer. Basically, the computer terminal looks like combination of typewriter and television screen. The keyboard is that channel whereby the user can communicate to the computer- and the plasma screen which looks like a television tube is the source from which the user gets information from the computer. The information appearing on the screen can be either print or graphic, and with some computer terminals, there is a light-sensitive pen that the user can touch against the screen as a means of responding to information generated and presented by the computer. The computer terminal is also capable of producing hard copy The librarian's prime task is to select, or contribute to the selection of. programs that will be stored in the computer for patron use. Most of these computers are extremely easy to operate and require very little instruction-usually a few typewritten directions will suffice. The computer can also be used to handle administrative and record keeping functions.

Filmstrip is another significant category. A filmstrip is a continuous strip of photographic film containing a series of still pictures intended to be viewed separately. Filmstrips can be either captioned or uncaptioned. They are primarily available in a 35-mm half. single, or double frame formal (half frame and single frame are synonyms companies now have filmstrips available in a 16-mm formal. On occasion, books are accompanied with short strips, which are small filmstrips usually only 8-10 frames in length.

Sound by either disc record or audiotape (reel or cassette). A few years ago, a filmstrip was marketed with the sound information right on the filmstrip, but it never gained wide commercial acceptance.

A very wide term which has become more popular during recently is 'kit'. A universally accepted definition of the term kit is lacking because producers of kits do not use the term the same way. A kit is a collection or package of two or more items on a particular topic. Therefore, if a producer packages of two or more items on and calls it a kit it should be so classified. As an example, a producer will package several filmstrips and call it a kit, whereas another producer will call it a series. Usually a kit must be purchased as a complete unit- but a series of filmstrips can be purchased separately. Perhaps a true kit would be a multimedia kit, which contains a variety of media (books, recording, filmstrips, guides, dittoes, etc.) or realia (coins artifacts, minerals, etc.) dealing with a particular topic.

A map or chart is identified as a single unbound, discrete item capable of being examined as a complete entity, Maps and charts vary in size, from items that can be held in one hand, to panels mounted on an entire wall. Maps are usually identified as to type and purpose (political, geographic, topographic, equal area, polar, etc.) Some maps are made of paper and can be folded when stored. Still other maps are backing, and are intended to be rolled when stored. Still other maps are textured or three dimensional and made of plastic. Charts could be pictorial, diagrams, floor plans, blueprints layouts- or flowcharts. Atlases are actually books of maps and as such could be categorized as books. Also, globes although often considered maps, are really models of the earth, satellites solar system, or stars

As we have already discussed about films and motion pictures, these require viewing and possible listening equipment. Although motion pictures are available in many formats, libraries are usually involved with 16-mm, super 8-mm, and standard or regular 8-mm formats. (Commercial theatres use 35-mm, and 70 mm formats.) Films are available with sound tracks or silent, and the sound track can be either magnetic or optical.

Pamphlet is another kind of the print on paper. The term pamphlet varies in definition but it is generally an unbound work of one or more pieces of paper stapled together. Pamphlets usually provide information on topics of interest; they are not intended to be exhaustive in their contents, but to provide the reader with some specific information. Pamphlets vary in size from small foldouts to stapled materials printed in a variety of sizes. A pamphlet usually contains less than 50 pages.

Periodicals are not to be confused with pamphlets. Although in physical appearance they may look like some pamphlets, they are published on a regular, or periodical, basis, identified by title, and classified by volume, issue and date, It may be said that a periodical has continuity Incidentally, accumulated periodicals can be bound, and many of them are available in microform.

Pictures differ from maps and charts in that they are either photographs of objects or works of art that are drawn or painted. Pictures are available as photographs, various kinds of graphics, and illustrations. A librarian can inexpensively build a fine collection of pictures by clipping them out of discarded publications. Often these clipped visuals can be mounted on cardboard to give them a quality worthy of display. The end product of this effort of clipping, mounting, and gathering various kinds of pictures will be a picture file if continually developed and built on a picture file can become a compendium of visuals used for study, the development of visual statements or stories, or pure esthetic appreciation. This is best exemplified by the compilation of pictures for use as study prints, accompanied by textual explanatory materials on the subject. This is somewhat different from using art prints (discussed previously-original art or reproductions, framed or unframed) for circulation to patrons for display and appreciation in their own homes.

Programmed instruction includes materials designed to instruct the learner in a prescribed sequence of (a) surplus (giving information), (b) response (providing the learner with an opportunity to answer or respond), and (c) reinforcement (giving the learner immediate feedback on his or her responses). Programmed instruction can be either of lineal or of the branching type. It is available in linear texts and scramble texts for use in teaching machines, or in a program to be used with a computer. Programmed instruction can be subcategorized as anything from a book to a host of media, both print and non-print.

Real things and models cover a multitude of materials and can vary in size from very small to extremely large. Real things, also called realia, include items such as live animals, animal specimens, minerals, plants, manufactured items arid works of art. A model, on the other hand, is a representation of a real thing that has been enlarged or reduced, a cutaway or cross-section simplified or modified for easier viewing or understanding, or even a replica blowup, miniaturization, or diorama. A replica, of course, could be classified as a real thing in some cases.

Recordings require listening equipment. Audiotapes are available in various speeds identified in inches per second (ips). Recordings can be monaural, stereophonic, stereophonic, or quadraphonic. The major types of information found on recordings are music, storytelling, reading, speeches, recitals and sound effects. Disk also require listening equipment. Disc recordings are available in various speeds or revolutions per minute (rpm). The speeds are 16 2/3, 45, and 78 rpm. The 16 2/3-rpm record is called a transcription, and 78-rpm recordings are obsolete and no longer in production. Information found on disc recordings is of basically the same type as that found on audiotape recordings. Recordings can be monaural, stereophonic, or quadraphonic.

Videotapes require viewing and listening equipment. Videotape recordings are becoming more available to libraries. Libraries favor the helical scan format to the quadruplex format because helical scan equipment costs a fraction of the quadruplex equipment. Videotapes are available in open reel or cassette and range from ¼ to 2 inches (0.6 to 5.1cm) in width. Recent developments have been made with videodiscs, and they will soon be available in libraries. Videotape programs can be purchased commercially or produced locally.

Simulations and games are being packaged to provide the patron with a wide range of learning and recreational activities. They can be as simple as a printed scenario and as complex as boxed with playing boards, counters dice, spinning discs, etc. Simulations and games are intended to provide active participant behavior.

Slides require viewing equipment. Slides differ from filmstrips in that they are individually mounted photograph, and not placed on one continuous piece of film. In this way, they can be rearranged, augmented, and deleted. The prevalent size is 2 + 2 inches (5.1/5.1 vcm), which is a measurement of the entire slide including the mount. Greatest use of slides is in the area of local production and the visual arts architecture, sculpture, etc.).

Overhead transparencies are used extensively in education. The are usually mounted on 26-30 cm (10¼ - 11¾ inch) frames and contain a base transparency and possibly overlay transparencies. The major types of transparencies are clear acetate (on which information is drawn with a pen), thermal (heat process), and diazo (low-speed photographic). Polarized transparencies, through the use of special materials and equipment, give an illusion of motion when projected.

The above categories can, if needed, be expanded or reduced, depending on the type of bibliography being prepared. The list can serve as a classification guide in categorizing media. It can also be invaluable when the librarian must decide on exactly what kind of selection aid should be used in searching for a particular type of item.

Educational media contain a larger body of information in a condensed form. If a researcher gathers 100% of available information on his subject then only 10% of the information is used in the film, whether in the script itself or the commentary spoken over the film. Yet the script writer needs to be in command of the other 90% of information, to back him up with the necessary endorsement confirmation in support which he in order to be able to state with confidence that his information is complete and accurate.

In the words of Prof. Beverage "the visible information in a film- the information contained expressed in the story and stated in the dialogue and commentary- resemble the proportion of an iceberg which can be seen floating on the surface of the ocean. Only one eighth of the iceberg can be seen on the surface of the water- seven eighths of its bulk is below the surface and cannot be seen. This gives an analogy with the information contained of a film. Only a small proportion of the facts are literary seen or heard in such a presentation".

The major functions of an educational media library are, selection, acquisition, organization, processing and dissemination of information available in varied formats and specially their use in education. These functions are almost the same as in case of other libraries but the educational media libraries differ in approaches, performance and techniques adopted to process the educational materials.

Technology has brought crucial change in the pattern of generating and acquiring knowledge. Perhaps no other area of professions has buffeted in so short a time by the computer revolution as that of the educational media librarianship. The rapid emergence of multimedia, CD ROM materials as in its way defined the change from analog to digital systems and along with the change has come with increasingly pervasive emphasis on computer based technologies and multimedia design and access. Moreover, digital network technology that is the Internet, digital satellite system etc. and the soon to be universal High Definition Television (HDTV) has further radicalized the information field.

Now, seemingly for the very first time, librarians are not only selecting text, data, still and moving images and audiovisual materials from various sources near and far. they are also customizing these sources for information seekers. In short, they are finding themselves in the position of creating new information products and avenues and adding to the knowledge base. The new situation has obviously called for drastic changes in the training of media librarians and also for organization and management of media libraries. The revised ALA standard for accreditation broadened the academic rubric for library programmes from the old librarianship to the new library and information studies in 1992.

The first major function of a library is the acquisition of library materials. Acquisition involves the process of selection, ordering and payment. It also includes the conditions of use of the resources purchased for the library as well as maintaining the record of the items purchased and weeding them out when necessary. Mason Robinson stressed the following points for adding a new media format to ones library:

1. Economy of scale; the library can only make this decision after needs assessment and specific tracking of customer needs
2. Financial support of the institution, which includes budget approval for software and hardware and additional staff and their training, if needed
3. Product sufficiency and equality
4. Equipment, the product should be readily available and have sufficient tech support for library use
5. The actual use that the product will have by the users. The company should have a good history of supporting its products in direct proportion to the number of users expected to use the product.

Mason Robinson has outlined an easy guide for development of the collection of educational media and suggests the following points to be considered:

1. Include the library's mission statement.
2. Give the library's composition, including the size and characteristics of the students body, the age group served, the ethnic facial make up and the language spoken.
3. Identify the community's economic base as it affects the school curriculum
4. Shows that the library's budget is in percentage of all totals in the budget and is directly proportional to the circulation percentage.
5. State who is responsible for the selection.
6. Shows that criteria will be used to select these materials.
7. Delineate the make up of the collection showing what it contains, where or not it is adult or children's material, popular or documentary/informational material, what interest and needs of the population it serves and whether there are any special collections,
8. Address what formats are offered, what circulation restrictions are, including length of loan.
9. Include how many of formats may be borrowed, what the late, damage or lost fees are and whether or not the collection can be inter library loaned
10. Clearly state access issues including the provision of circulation to minors, the freedom to view statement and the procedure to follow challenged material.
11. Add a readily understandable periodic collection evaluation with a clearly delineated de-accession process.

Merle J. Styhoff of the University of Pennsylvania has given a list of the selection tolls for the educational media including video and CD ROMs. Some of the general resources include:

1. The TIA film and video guide booklist
2. Booker's complete video directory
3. Catalog of captioned educational video and films
4. CD ROM finder
5. CD ROMs in print
6. Children's Software Finder
7. Children's video reports
8. Best of the best for children
9. Educational film and video locator
10. Roger Elberts video communion
11. Faxon's guide to electronic media
12. Film and video finder
13. Gate dictionary of databases
14. Best videos for children and young adults
15. CD ROMs source book
16. Lender's film and video review
17. Publishers weekly
18. RLIN school library journal
19. Video librarian
20. The video source hooks

Styhoff has given about forty other books, other journals and CD ROM titles, which are helpful in selection of the educational media.

In India, there are three major networks which are engaged in production, and distribution of educational media. 'The oldest among the production agencies is the network of the National Council of Educational Research and Training (NCERT) through which its subordinate agency i.e. the Central Institute of Educational Technology (CIET) brings out catalogue of their holdings. CIET has regional centers in Lucknow and Simla, which also produce educational software. The productions brought out by CIET are contrarily listed in their catalogue and are marketed through them.

Consortium for Educational Communication distributes their audio and video cassettes through their agency, The Educational Aid International. New Delhi. They have also published their catalogue separately for the various major disciplines of study. About all the productions of the Educational Media Research Centres (EMRC) and Mass Communication Research Centre are available through Educational Aid International on the uniform terms and conditions

It has been found that adequate selection tools are not available in the country. The catalogues of producers are still the only solution for selection of educational media. There has been no coordination among the similar agencies for bringing out a comprehensive catalogue of the available resources. On the other hand, a lot has been done on deciding the formats of entries for the computerization of media libraries and bringing out a union catalogue of all the productions contributed by EMRCs. The main sources of selection of educational media in the country are the following:

(a) Catalogues of producing agencies

(b) Catalogues of distributors

(c) Reviews as appeared in the print media

(d) Stores available online

The following should be the conditions for purchase of the educational media specially, video and CD ROMs;

(a) Should state clearly what access rights are being acquired by the licensee for permanent use of the content or access time only for as defined period of time.

(b) Should recognize and not restrict or abrogate the rights of the licensee or its, user community permitted under copyright law. The licensee should make clear to the licensor those uses critical to its particular users, including but not limited to printing, downloading and copying.

(c) Should recognize the intellectual property rights of both the licensee and the licensor.

(d) Should not hold the licensee liable for unauthorized uses of licensed resources by its users as long as the licensee has implemented reasonable and appropriate methods to notify its user community of use restrictions.

(e) Should be willing to undertake appropriate method to enforce the terms of access to a licensee resource.

(f) Should fairly recognize those access enforcement obligations, which, the licensee is able to implement without unreasonable burden.

(g) The enforcement does not violate the property and confidentiality of authorized users.

(h) Should be responsible for establishing policies that create an environment in which authorized users make appropriate use of licensed resources and for carrying out due process when it appears that a uses may violate the agreement.

(i) Should require the licensor to give the licensee notice of any suspected or alleged license violation that come to the attention of the licensor and allows a responsible time for the licensee to investigate and take corrective action, if appropriate.

(j) Should not require the use of the authentication system that is a barrier to access by authorized users

(k) When permanent use of the resource has been licensed, should allow the licensee to copy data for the purpose of preservation and /or the creation of a usable archival copy.

(1) The terms of license should be considered fixed at the time the license is signed by both parties. If the terms are subject to change, the agreement should require the licensor or licensee to notify the party in a timely and reasonable fashion of any

such change before they are implemented, and permit either party to terminate the agreement if the changes are not acceptable.

(m) Should require the licensor to defend, indemnify and hold the licensee harmless for any action based on a claim that use of resources in accordance with the license infringes and patent copyright, trade mark or trade secrets of any third party.

(n) The routine collection of used data by either party to a licensee agreement should be predicated up on disclosure of such collection activities to the other party and must respect laws and instructional policies regarding confidentiality and privacy.

(o) Should not require the licensee to adhere to unspecified terms in a separate agreement between the licensor and the third party unless the terms are fully.

The first major shift for libraries from a traditional medium was witnessed when libraries adopted educational technology. It started from the capability of mechanical duplication of documents and ended up with its delivery in different formats. The micrographs of documents led to reduction in size and provided mobility, which facilitated dissemination of information. Precious holdings were transformed into microfiches for consultation and preservation for the posterity.

In India, number of governmental and private agencies emerged to augment the process of production of educational software in varied formats. The Department of Teaching Aids, which is now known as the Central Institute of Educational Technology of the National Council for Educational Research and Training, New Delhi started in late forties. A large number of educational audio and video programs were produced by them, which are telecast now through the radio and television. In fact, television was introduced in India in 1959 as a pilot project of UNESCO to impart education. It proved a grad success and paved a way for its farther expansion.

The decade of 1980's saw very significant developments for the universities in India. The University Grants Commission launched the INSAT TV PROJECT from the Mass Communication Research Centre of the Jamia Millia Islamia, New Delhi in 1984. A year later, the Indira Gandhi National Open University and the Central Institute of Educational Technology were also founded with multimedia approach in instruction. Then syllabi based educational audio and video programmes were produced by these agencies, which go on the air almost every day.

In fact, there is hardly any university that provides library services based on educational media to its users in an organized way whereas it is not a difficult and costly affair as before. The programs are available at such a low price that they can easily be afforded by even colleges. The Government of India has also promoted the use of audiovisuals among universities by allowing the investment of funds available for books and journals for purchase of the audiovisual programmes. The one time expenditure on equipment may be the only problem but it is also true that there are occasions when special grants are provided to the universities for modernization of the libraries services. Moreover, there are funds on discretion of the university authorities that can be utilized to start such services at a convenient time.

There are many reasons, for the popularity of films. In the process of education, the superordinate among the curricular components is the 'objective~'. The materials, methods and evaluation schemes are subordinate. The nature of materials applied in education should be such that they are effective means to achieve the set objectives. The main limitation with us is that the Indian society is not fully equipped to transform the system as it calls for a number of pre-requisites. That is why even today the most prevalent educational materials in our country are in the print medium. The infrastructure is developing fast. 'Television is entering the households even in the remotest areas. Dish Antennas and Cable TVs can be seen in the urban as well as the sub-urban localities. The Government of India is also inclined to dedicate a separate channel of Doordarshan to the educational broadcasts. The 'Countrywide Classroom' telecast in Hindi in addition to its English programs.

There are few agencies in the country dealing with the production and distribution of the educational films, agencies like the National Education and Information Films Ltd., Bombay. Some organizations market their own productions on demand. Selection can be made from the catalogues of the production agencies or from some other reference sources like the Video Source Book or from the lists of the distributors itself Some periodical publications carry reviews on motion pictures. Even in Indian publications we come across such references. Once selected, ordering and receiving is not a problem if the films have to be procured locally. But we always need films from the foreign countries for the specialized groups of learners. For this, we have no other way but to import the films.

The import policy for educational films is quite cumbersome. For granting clearance to a consignment coming from abroad, Customs authorities have a twofold function to perform; (a) to see whether the import is permitted under Import Trade Control Regulation laid down by the Ministry of Commerce, and (b) to assess Import Duty as prescribed by the Ministry of Finance Notification No. 305/87-Cus, where under educational videos imported for a university or college are exempted from levy of duty. As regards the first aspect necessary Import Trade Control Regulations appear in the Import Policy Book. The 1990-93 Import Policy Book provides for the import of educational films/videos under Open General Licence under two different sections.

Serial No. 36 of Appendix 6, List 8, Part ii appearing on

page 241 where under import of educational and instructional films or videos is allowed freely by all persons provided the films/videos imported are certified as 'Predominantly Educational" (PE) by the Central Board of Film Certification (CBFC). Serial No. 7 of Appendix 6 (Page 173) allows import of educational films or videos freely by all recognized educational institutions and government departments subject to Condition No. 41 appearing on page 188 that the films/videos imported are Predominantly Educational by the Central Board of Film Certification.

One fails to understand that when under the provision cited under (1) above, all persons (term covers recognized educational institutions and government departments, etc. also) are allowed to import educational films/videos provided the same are certified as 'PE' by CBFC, why separate provision cited at (b) above had to be made for the same purpose, specially for educational institutions and government departments and that too on the same conditions of 'PE' certificate being obtained from CBFC.

It appears that the condition of obtaining 'PE' certificate from CBFC under provision (b) above has been inserted inadvertantly as otherwise there was no need to have a separate provision for educational institutions and government departments.

Recognized educational institutions and government departments should be considered competent enough to certify the 'PE' nature of a motion picture as they all have subject experts on their staff and hence there should be no need for them to have to approach CBFC for such certification since after all CBFC itself issues certificates only at the recommendations of two of their panel members drawn from the public life and who are usually not subject experts.

Further procedural formalities involved in obtaining CBFC certificates like submitting applications, arranging of screenings under custom escorts and so forth are too cumbersome and obviously unnecessary to be gone through for a recognised educational institution or a government department. Being themselves the actual users of the materials, they should be exempted from being required to obtain 'PE' certificate from CBFC. In fact, the concerned institutions and/or department should be considered as equally, if not more competent to judge the 'PE' nature of the motion picture: required by them.

The films are treated as feature films in India whose import is allowed with very heavy import duty. An educational institution cannot afford to pay such duty. The cassettes solely meant for the education of students in the art of film production be allowed to be imported like books atleast for the educational institutions engaged in the art of educational media production.

In India, the main difficulty in import of the educational media is the fear of commercial exploitation But as far as their utility in education is concerned. It would be unfair to deny access to the students and researchers. While students of any discipline in the country have access to the print media, specially, books and journals of their choice they should also have equal opportunity to get benefited out of the new educational media. The literature of the various languages and their celebrated literary figures such as from Shakespeare to Marlowe in case of English, till modem time can be purchased from the market or ordered from abroad, the students and their parent institutions are precluded from seeing these cassettes of masterpieces of science and other subjects of study. The main obstacle in their in the import is the provision in import policy.

The Government of India allows import of the 'Pre dominantly educational films' as certified by the Central Board of Film Certification (CBFC) But in view of the Central Board of Film Certification, the only film. which can be certificates as pre-dominantly educational could be documentaries Films of all type including feature films if they are required for the educational institutions should be allowed to be imported just as the departments of literature in the institutions a are free to import books for the.

It appears that the condition of obtaining "ore dominantly educational" nature of motion pictures for the educational institutions as they all have subject experts on their staff and hence there should be no need for them tc have to approach CBFC for such certifications since after all CBFC itself issues certificates only at the recommendations of two of their panel members drawn from the public life and who are not actually not subject experts. Further procedural formalities involved in obtaining CBFC certificates like submitting applications, arrangement of screening under customs escorts and so forth a too cumbersome and obviously unnecessary to be gone for the recognized educational institutions or a government department. Being themselv :s the actual users of materials, they should be exempted from being required to obtain "PE" certificate from CBFC. In fact, the concerned institutions/departments should be considered as equally if not more competent to judge the "PF" nature of motion pictures required by them.

In the past, the cost of educational media specially, celluloid film was very high and the reason for it was the escalation in the cost of raw stock being distributed by the Hindustan Photo Films and also the processing charges. The arrival of video recording system has changed the scene drastically. It made possible the price cut to the extent of about ten times. Not only the production cost has declined but also the price of the finished products dropped down miraculously. The pricing structure offered by Educational International. New Delhi is very attractive. Similarly all government aided institutions in the country offer their productions at subsidized rates.

Library materials are expected to be used as widely as possible. The understanding reached between the distributor and the library authority is already clear on this issue before materializing the formalities of purchase. There are many ways and options adopted for the use and the conditions for it are usually laid down in the agreement.

Julia Gammon (1999) has laid down some 'bottom line considerations' for use of the educational media.

(a) Inclusive enough to cover all authorized clients and patron for the library. Any term related to users must be including those in other branches.

(b) The library will determine the authorized site issues to ensure inclusion of distance education.

(c) The library will differentiate use of technology

(d) The library will insist on predated refund if otherwise excluded.

(e) The library will not accept one-sided agreement.

(f) The library must use materials inside the classrooms

(g) The library materials must be able to circulate, if appropriate format.

(h) The database of serials articles must have the same privilege for Inter Library Loan as subscription.

(i) The library will provide reasonable effort to notify patron of use conditions and will participate in monitoring uses but not at the inconvenience of staff.

(j) The library will enter into agreements, but not seek them out. Responsibility for seeking agreement rests with the producer or the vendor

(k) The library has right to reproduce, prepare derivative list, distribute through circulation and other loans, use in classroom, use in performance etc.

(l) The library will comply with and insist on fair use of clauses.

(m) The library will determine authorized use of a producer

(n) The library will seek archival rights to maintain primer access.

The task of collection development for the educational media is different unlike the other library practices of information management. It needs specialized provisions and skill.

7

Organization of Library Resources

The basic principles of organization and managements of the educational media in libraries are almost the same as in case of the print media, but the educationists generally do not associate libraries with the non-print media in the same context as they relate them with the print media. The reason for it lies in absence of standardized and reliable system for management of the information contained in documents. In this direction, efforts are being made and they can prove to be fruitful if the expertise gained in libraries is applied properly to management of the new information media.

The management of media collections depends upon the schemes of classification, cataloguing codes, assignment of proper subject headings and the other library techniques that are employed for organization of the print based media but with certain modalities required as per the special needs of the collections. The following are the library techniques which may be helpful in this task.

CLASSIFICATION

The information has no value unless it is organized to retrieve right information for right user at right time. Classification is necessary for organization of library materials. Even in the present information era such services are necessary for the users to get the desired materials easily and in a well-organized way.

Classification has many new roles to play in designing, searching and managing an electronic database. The use of automatically constructed classification is still a subject of investigation. Although many techniques have been developed yet the successful implementation of such techniques has not been made possible till this date. Automatic classification is still a goal. But as far as the classification of the educational media is concerned it is almost the same as applicable in case of the other media. The various schemes of classification available through out the world are used to classify various types of documents.

Audiovisual materials are difficult to scan without the aid of machinery. Invention of machinery is necessary between a user and information, which is a time consuming task hence, these non browsable material requires detailed classification. Books are generally arranged on shelves in a classified order. But tapes are arranged according to the Accession Numbers with the reason that each tape contains programmes on different subjects. Same tapes are also sometimes reused for recording another programmes on a different subject.

Some tape libraries do follow classification pattern for the maintenance of tapes. To ascertain relation between the subject content of various tapes, the classification is a must. If a standard classification scheme is adopted, then the possibilities of exchange data and formation of national databank of the audiovisual programmes is greater. Standard classification and cataloguing systems help much for integration of material.

Various schemes of classification like Dewey Decimal Classification. Universal Decimal Classification. Library of Congress Classification and Colon Classification are in use in order to allow a user to know about the availability of materials through its classes and subjects. The idea of a system of classification or indexing is to be able to retrieve relevant information with accuracy and minimum delay.

The introduction of a classification scheme depends upon the size of the collection of a library. Larger the collection, greater is the need for detailed classification. Classification brings the like materials together and also establishes relationship between the various segments of the contents of documents. The classification schemes are based on notation- either numerical or alphabetical or a combination of both.

A good classification scheme has the following properties:

(a) Systematic proceeding from general to particular.

(b) As complete as possible and covers the whole field of its given subject.

(c) Indicative of the relationship between subjects and permits classification from different points of view.

(d) Expansive and flexible in plan and use.

(e) Supplied with alphabetical index to the notation.

CATALOGUING

In the present time with advancement of modern technology, the varieties of educational materials have increased such as transparencies, computer disks, TV films, laser cards, optical discs etc. It is growing at a very fast speed. It requires special storage conditions and effective bibliographical control since all these materials have their place and importance and they also require proper organization and management. Therefore, the collections are being managed as per the established practice of library science with local variation depending upon many factors.

Cataloguing is a listing of all library collection with complete bibliographical details. Cataloguing helps in the process of containing relevant information from the collection of the library. Library catalogues can assist the users in the following manners:

(1) To enable a person to find materials of which (a) author is known (b) the title is known and (c) the subject is known.

(2) They show what the library has (a) by giving the author (b) given the subject and (c) in given type of literature.

(3) To assist in the choice of materials (a) as to its edition and (b) as to its character.

The foregoing characteristics of a library catalogue were given by Charles Ammi Cutter in 1876 and after more than 100 years it is still valid.

There is really no substitute for viewing A/V film for cataloguing, classification indexing and abstracting. However due to various constraints i.e. manpower, time, availability of viewing machines etc., the cataloguer has to depend on the information provided by the production company.

Films are important sources of information. With the increase of television channels the amount of film being produced is increasing day by day. It needs proper cataloguing for optimum utilization of the resources. The films received in the libraries are on varying subjects and a number of enquiries are received regarding their use,

The access point for catalogue of films is generally the title since it is regarded as a team work. Therefore. title is of utmost importance for the cataloguers.

The educational media due to their peculiar inherent format, very frequently pose serious problems in their arrangement, cataloguing and retrieval of information, hence the cataloguer may encounter the following possible problems:

(a) Information may be difficult to obtain from the documents to be catalogued than with conventional documents having title page.

(b) Information collected from one source in the document may differ with that obtained from the other source of the document.

(c) It may be harder to reach the cataloguing decisions with reference to the choice of access points.

(d) Information about physical description of different types of media definitely creates hurdles for cataloguer rather than the conventional documents.

(e) It is very difficult to obtain information through the naked eyes as it requires special equipment.

Every code of cataloguing attempts to deal with the special problems posed by the educational media. The most famous is among them is the Anglo American Cataloguing Rules 2. It is divided in two parts i.e. Part 1 Description of materials including the Non Book Materials (NBM) in which chapter 6 and 7 deal with the rules for cataloguing of sound recordings and motion pictures and video recordings respectively. Whereas Part-2 consists of choice of Access Points for the conventional documents and non print media, Headings for Persons and Corporate Bodies etc.

Many of the catalogue codes have been based on the practical experience of the librarians as far as the cataloguing of films is concerned. They cooperate and try to agree to the general rules or practices. Various rules, which are in practice. In Library of Congress Rules, rules are divided into 4 main sections dealing with title catalogue, News film catalogue, index and style. The Library of Congress Rules were designed for general collection of films and to meet the needs of general collections of films in the United States. The first section deals with the choice of entry, second with imprint and the third with physical description.

Anglo American Cataloguing Rules are specifically formulated to meet the needs of the multimedia library collections in general libraries and resource centers. They can be adopted to the needs of specialized institutions and single medium collections. It may be necessary for certain compromises to be made for designing a set of rules for multimedia collections, the media are not similar and cannot all be treated in exactly the same way. Local variations and users requirements are important factors in adopting any rules and these factors have to be given weightage in preparing rules for cataloguing of the library collections.

Video recordings can be on film, tape or cassette. The video films are known and recognized by title and hence the main entry for these films is made under the title. The added entries can be made on the other aspects of film making e.g. producers, actors, cameramen, directors etc.

The information given on a catalogue entry for a document can be divided into three areas:

(a) Heading

(b) Description

(c) Subject Description

The procedure adopted for video programmes is very much like news film cataloguing procedures with some modifications to suit video materials. The entry should include all possible details including color, playing time in minutes and seconds, the video size, production date. Its diameter may be used to add information on the play back speed. As videotapes have their format given reel or cassette and manufacturing company, the trade names and numbers are required to be given for the scanning system. In addition it is necessary to mention the gauge of the tape for there are more than five gauges in use. The length of tape and playing time, the number of tracks, the generations of copies and whether it is a master or show copy is to be provided in case of video recordings.

INDEXING

Index is a systematic guide to the items of collection or the concept derived in a known searchable order with reference to show where each item indexed is located. The purpose of index is to locate or to retrieve the needed item or concept in that collection.

There are many types of indices. The most common we find is at the back of the book.

(a) Index is a guide to name, places, item, concept etc. in a document or documents.

(b) The items and concepts in the index are arranged systematically in an alphabetical order, and

(c) There are references to show where each of the items is located in the document or documents.

Subject Headings

The need for proving subject approach to the documents made the determining of an appropriate subject heading necessary, in cataloguing as well as in indexing. However, most of the documents have composite subjects consisting of a number of components e.g. selection of periodicals in the university libraries in India. Here the subjects heading can be (i) selection of periodicals (ii) selection of periodicals in university libraries.

Since the subject of such documents cannot be expressed by a single term therefore a number of terms are to be used.

In place of a natural language the indexing language is used to represent the subject contents so that a searchable file is constructed for easy and quick retrieval. This is done because (i) the vocabulary of the indexing languages is exact and precise (ii) there is a control over the use of synonyms and homonyms and (iii) it is helpful in file organization. The following are the popular, important and generally accepted lists of subject heading/thesaurus:

(a) Sears List of Subject Headings.

(b) Library of Congress List of Subject Headings.

(c) NASA Thesaurus

Subject headings play a role of catalyst in reflecting the thought content of the documents, thereby enhancing the potentiality of retrieving the relevant documents by using the subject approach. Subject headings provide speed in the access to the collection of a library and also make the services more effective and accurate. In other words, the better the selection of subject headings, the more efficiently the documents are retrieved.

The assignment of subject headings to the educational media follows almost the same principles as applied in case of the print media. It is particularly important to integrate and incorporate provisions for assigning similar subject heading to all type of materials available in a particular library so that the researcher may find all type of documents at one place in the catalogue.

The educational media very often concentrate on very small aspects of large subject, which the cataloguer may not find in the list of the subject headings that should be used to reflect the content judiciously. In such a situation, the cataloguer should be generous in adding new subject. There are many form headings that apply to the educational as well as print media equally such as bibliographical film, comedy, television programmes and science fiction comic books.

The following are the main issues in assigning subject headings to the educational media:

(a) Sometimes, subject headings used tend to be over broad.

(b) Search of the print version of the reference using subject approach is unlikely to find other media.

(c) The specific subject heading assigned to a document normally follow the principle for specific entry.

(d) Poor subject headings may mean incorrect headings

(e) Title alone is not sufficient to reflect the hidden content of the media.

(f) Print counterparts of the media materials may not be retrieved.

8

INFORMATION SOURCES AND SYSTEMS

The most common form of educational media is the educational film. Educational films are short duration films normally running from 2 to 30 minutes. Some of the institutions consider up to 45 minutes films in this category. They are different from the commercial, entertainment and developmental films in respect of their contents. The educational films are solely meant for education and there is no expectation from them for generation of financial resources. The educational films can be categorized according to their target audience. In India, films of different categories are being produced by different agencies. Films for the primary classes are normally produced by the Educational Television, a division of Doordarshan.

Information is the basic resource for a filmmaker. Unless and until mastery is obtained over a subject on which someone intends to produce a film the work cannot be carried out satisfactorily. This has special significance for short educational films. In the words of a renowned documentary film maker of our own times Prof. James A Beverage "The visible information in a film, the information content expressed in the story and stated in the dialogues and commentary resembles the proportion of an iceberg which can be seen floating on the surface of the ocean. Only one eighth, we are told, of the iceberg can be seen above the surface of the water — seven-eighths of its bulk is below the surface and can not be seen. This gives us an analogy with the information contents of our films. Only a small proportion of the facts are literally seen or heard in the film presentation. But a much larger body has been absorbed and studied by researcher". *(Script Writing for Short Film.* Paris, UNESCO, 1975) p-8

The vast amount of information gathered in varied forms of documents is the raw material for a production. It should be used with great care. The filmmaker should have firm control over all the resources in order to avoid any confusion as the arrangement and presentation of information in an imperfect way can lead to convey different meanings. This reminds of a short film the Eye of the Beholder' wherein a particular event means differently to all the five persons who saw the event. It is worth mentioning here that none of the beholders perceived the real message. There is always scope for confusion in case the information is not placed in a proper perspective.

Film production on celluloid is a very costly and time taking process, which has now almost succumbed to video. Video has revolutionized the world of motion pictures because of its instant playback facility and the lower cost of production. Films having higher resolution are being produced in many video formats. The problems in preservation have also been overcome by the advent of digital technology. Images and sound can now be pre-served for hundreds of years without involvement of much care for them as in case of celluloid films.

Film production, whether on celluloid or video, is a costly affair. The shooting of sequences invites for much pains and financial resources; therefore, there is always a desire to preserve these sequences and reuse them whenever possible in future productions. One can hardly find any production agency where the footage is not retained in the hope of utilization but it is seldom used properly, and the main reason for this is generally the lack of proper information systems.

SOURCES OF INFORMATION

The filmmakers adopt a multi-media approach. They need information in varied forms and at different stages of work. The ideas are needed for selection of the production themes. A newspaper having altogether different stories or a news bulletin can invoke the hidden desire of doing a programme on a particular topic but only a very few film makers have the privilege of selecting the themes for their productions. Normally, the production themes are assigned to them by the sponsoring body. They may sometimes have a broad idea given by the sponsors which can further be elaborated and tested in accordance with the suitability. The factors like the expenditure involved, the availability of subject experts and the convenience in shooting the sequences are equally important. Once the theme of a production is finalized, the process of production begins. The first step is to try to know more about the subject; to absorb the maximum information available; to digest it and transform it into the language of words and pictures. This is the ultimate goal of a film maker. The sources of information thus needed can be categorized as print, visual, audio and electronic.

Print Sources

After finalizing the topic of production the first step should be to consult a dictionary or an encyclopaedia. A dictionary will be too general a tool for a person having a professional background. Alternatively, encyclopaedia have comprehensive coverage on all the subjects. Specialized encyclopaedia can be consulted depending upon the specific needs. If someone intends to produce a programme on diodes it would always be advisable to search for the desired information in an encyclopaedia on science. Once a complete picture of the theme is constructed, one should move to the current sources for data or relevant statistics since the production has to be related with the time and space. Books, periodicals, articles, research publications and press clippings can be consulted to elaborate and present a comprehensive coverage on the topic of production. It is worth mentioning here that press clippings, barring a few having archive value, lose their currency after two years of their publications and generally the topics covered in newspapers are transformed into books or atleast they are published in editorials of the periodicals. But still a news story on paper can be shot for a production to take back the audience to the time when the incident took place.

Visual Sources

Most essential of the primary sources of information about the educational films are the actual programmes available on the subject. One of the first steps for a film-maker is to know before starting on production whether his intended subject has already been covered by other films and if so where those films can be hired from for review. Such information is not always easy to come by but it pays if somebody attempts. For educational films in India, there are sources to determine it. Now, union catalogues of EMRCs, AVRCs and MCRC are available from the Consortium for Educational Communication, New Delhi. It is expected to update the records electronically every month in the near future. In addition, the catalogues of CIET, SIETs and ETV productions of Doordarshan can also be seen. IITs also produce films on scientific and technical subjects. The search can be made keeping in view the subject of programme and the level of audience for whom the film is going to be produced. The films thus reviewed can give ideas on treatment of a subject by different filmmakers and to ultimately decide the method of presentation. Some of the shots may also be relevant and useful and they can be used in the productions but the permission of the copyright holder is essential before using shots from others' films.

Film catalogues can only give a broad idea of the contents of a particular film. It can be known better by running a film on player at high speed. The editing mechanics have this facility but still it is a lengthy process. In India, the largest producing agency of educational films for higher education is the Consortium for

Educational Communication working under the University Grants Commission.

The films produced by the government agencies are now distributed by The Educational Book Distributors, New Delhi against a nominal price. Their catalogue gives a very broad idea about the programmes in around 100 words only. So far there is no established practice of assigning Keywords or standard subject headings to the productions so that one can retrieve information on the desired shots or atleast about the complete productions.

In the film and television libraries, the range of materials is very high and if the information systems are proper and one searches for long enough there may not be any difficulty in getting the desired information. But there are some shots that are impossible or atleast extremely costly to secure. News departments usually have special libraries, which take care of the archive materials and supply them to the department when it is needed again. But it is for the filmmaker to make sure that the desired shot is available in the library during the early stages of planning for a production. In India stock shots can be purchased from many agencies now. Doordarshan preserves the shots of archival value, which are available on payment per minute. Similarly, there are other agencies, private as well as governmental who sell their stock shots. The Mass Communication Research Centre at Jamia Millia Islamia can also be contacted for the desired shots. But still there has not been any organized effort in compilation of their reference sources and distribution. Obviously, there are more difficulties in using archive shots in video than in film and it is because of the prevailing crises of standardization in video. A shot on VHS will lose its quality if transferred onto U-Matic as it has a superior quality hardware. Likewise it is not advisable to use a U-Matic shot in a Betacam production. It is not always necessary to prove that the particular shot is an integral part of a film. Sometimes the message is more important than the medium.

Audio Sources

Just as a filmmaker selects and uses visuals already available, he or she may also use the prerecorded music. The choosing of an appropriate music is an art in itself. It is not permissible to take recordings from radio and TV and to use them freely. The recording of music is a costly affair as it involves musicians, composers and arrangers. It is always expected to pay royalty for the music and use it after. There are numerous agencies in India too where the desired music can be selected, no-table among them are All India Radio, Gramophone Company of India Ltd, Music Today of M/S Living Media India, etc. Another kind of sound used in productions is sound effect. They may be procured from the BBC or EMI or produced locally depending upon the nature of the event to be synchronized. Sound can also be selected from the completed film or video productions.

Electronic Sources

(a) Information Networks

The most significant electronic sources of information are the Information Networks and the CD-ROMs. One can search in a local environment through a Local Area Network or from the international databases sitting comfortably at his place of work by establishing contact with the host computer located in any part of the world. This is achieved with the help of a computer, a frequency modulator and the telecommunication links all connected together. Once the contact is established with any database, whether regional or international, the interaction may be followed for the desired information. These services are being offered now on commercial basis too. In order to ensure economy in search, the help of a professionally qualified person in the information area is obvious as the standard search terms arc coined to interact with the databases. Recent trends in assigning keywords and using uniform data input formats show signs of hope in this direction. If needed, the information thus retrieved can be downloaded from the host to the local computer and utilized whenever required.

(b) CD-ROMs

CD-ROMs no longer deal with storage and manipulation of the textual data. Now, they are invading the territories of audio and video with the same speed as of the print world. *(Educational Media International* March 1993). There are a number of information sources, which have directly emerged on CD-ROMs rather than on paper. Great economy is involved for libraries in opting for them. CD-ROM is particularly useful for larger libraries and research institutions. One may have reservations on installation of the CD-ROM facility in Indian circumstances because of the initial cost involved. But what is important is that it involves only one time expenditure on hardware and then the facility runs far cheaper. The *Encyclopaedia Britannica* is available on CD-ROM cheaper than on paper. This needs hardly one tenth of the expenditure to purchase it on CD ROM than on paper, which every moderate library is supposed to make. Further the search time is reduced miraculously. Hardly any major field of information remains untouched today by the invasion of CD-ROMs.

(c) Multi-media

Multimedia is the result of advancement in the compact disc-based technology. in the coming 10 years, this may supersede all the existing systems of storage and display of information because of its several advantages. One multi-media disc can contain more than 75,000 photographic images, more than 16 hours of audio and the equivalent of 30,000 pages of text (*AV Video* December 1992). One can imagine how economic it will be in terms of the space required for housing the equivalent information on paper. Further, the multi-media player which earlier consisted of several boxes including a monitor, a computer and a disc player can now be held comfortably in a briefcase. Such portable systems are already being marketed by Sony and Phillips Corporation. The titles available on multi-media discs now includes the general reference materials as well as the discs dealing with specialized disciplines. One such disc which became very popular in the academic circles is entitled 'AV Online' which can be of great use to the educational filmmakers. AV Online is a product of the National Information Centre for Educational Media. It is comprehensive database of educational audio-visual materials including video tapes, films, audio cassettes, filmstrips, etc. AV Online contains documentaries as well as instructional, informational and recreational programmes. Materials are in English, Spanish, French, German and 60 other languages. In India AV Online can be procured through Faxon Informatics Limited, Bangalore.

The advancements in technology have benefited the process of imparting education with the help of educational films. A film exploits the senses of sight and hearing by communicating messages in the forms of video and audio. The vast amount of information needed for production of a film is gathered from many sources. It seems that in the times to come the electronic sources will be put to greater use by the makers of educational films since these sources are capable of holding a larger body of information in varied forms of communication media.

INFORMATION SYSTEMS

Information can be available in any form of documents. The forms of documents have kept changing through out the history. After the invention of paper and the printing press the rate of generation of information grew enormously. As a result, methods to organize documents systematically and scientifically were evolved.

The technological developments in photography, sound recording and reproduction techniques and cinematography—a byproduct of the merger of photography and sound—gave birth to newer kinds of documents like photograph, microfilm, microfisches, gramophone records, sound spools, audiotapes, audiocassettes, discs, cinematographic film, video recordings, CD-ROMs, multimedia discs etc.

Media libraries hold the collections of many kinds of documents and generally organize them under one system of information. The concept of resource centre is being familiarized now and the libraries there are increasingly becoming a part of the resource centres. Both the media libraries and the resource centres are common as for the variety in their holdings is concerned. Both of them adopt one system of information for their collections. The difference is in the purpose of their services. A media library can be an open place for the public whereas as resource centre normally serves a particular organization with all it.', resources. Prof P N Kaula, a prominent contemporary librarian, refers to this change as a serious challenge for the profession. Librarians have to accept this and he ready to cope with the forthcoming trends of the new developments, in India too, some of the institutions like the National Institute of Fashion Technology and the Mass Communication Research Centre organize their resources under one system of information. Their collections include books, cassettes, films, press-clippings, photographs, costumes etc.

There are probably as many ways of organizing the documents as there are media libraries. In a particular media library, the emphasis can be on one or two types of materials while there may be general collections of many kinds of non-book materials. The major collections of the television production libraries are primarily based on videocassettes. They may also have music tapes and cassettes, slides, scripts and press-clippings, books and photographs. A common approach to organize them can be through their accession numbers since it is not advisable to shift these costly materials on the shelves all the times whenever a new document is added to the collection as it happens in case of the books which are arranged in a classified order. Films, cassettes, slides and discs can be damaged while shifted frequently Arrangement through accession numbers ensures a permanent place to a particular document and it is disturbed only when needed. Books can also be arranged in order of accession provided an on-line-information service is available to the users. This will prove an alternate to the classified search as computer can co-ordinate the concepts on its screen. An analytical scheme of classification will offer great facility by reversible as well as irreversible searches. The documents thus selected can be picked up from the shelves in a much shorter time than in a classified arrangement of books. This is particularly advantageous when the book collection of a library is not very large.

Computer has advantage over man in respect of speed, accuracy and memory. There was no wide spread use of computers in libraries in the early 70's and some of the services like on-line-information service were not known to the librarians. But even at that time the father of Library Science Drs S R Ranganathan perceived the potential of computer in advance. He kept abreast of progress in the 'Mechanization of Library Services' and in one of his lectures on "Impact of Electronics" at the first IASLIC conference he wrote for the librarians: "You are a growing organism. Therefore, you must grow with the world. The world has now entered the Electronic Age. You should use electronics to speed up work and to save man-power whenever practicable. In respect of finding documents for readers you should instruct Electronic Engineers to design a Doc-finder which will give speed without scarifying any of the essential human needs laid down by the forth Laws of Library Science". (Library Science Journal. June 1969; p 108)

A study on application of computers in libraries reveals that while processing 500 titles in a library manually as well as through computer, the difference in terms of the man hours required is around 1,000 and 65 hours respectively. (AGLIS Journal: April 1993). The major difference in the time required is due to computer's capability of manipulating the available data and retrieving that in different sequences. The information fed once only can be manipulated and retrieved indefinite times although the time taken in the feeding process for both the manual as well as the computer system is the same. In a manual system the same information is typed out or written the number of times it is needed. Its repetition in a library can be imagined from the fact that from the time of selection of a document to ordering, accessioning, cataloguing, circulation etc the same information is repeated again and again. A computer can not only provide a substitute to the problem of repetition but can also print any item of the information system viz. catalogue cards, book cards, tags, lists of documents and also the utilization reports.

Libraries of all kinds adopt common procedure in acquiring, cataloguing and circulation of documents. It is essential to know about these services and their computerization processes before proceeding further.

The basic functions covered under the acquisition system are: receiving recommendations of the documents to be procured and establishing that these documents are not already on order, preparing order notes to the suppliers for the documents ordered and not received, maintaining the accounts, entering the documents into records. The acquisition system must by accurate, timely, efficient and responsive to the demands of the library users. The computerization of the acquisition system involves creation and maintenance of two important files namely the document request file and the supplier's or agent's file. Apart from maintaining details separately, both the files can be 'mail-merged' to generate orders or for any sort of communication with the suppliers.

The next and the most important task in computerization of a media library is cataloguing. This provides the principal interface between the users of a library and its collection. The purpose of cataloguing is to make possible to the patrons, use of collection without going to the materials on the shelves sequentially each time a document is needed out of the collection. This means that adequate details about an individual document must be given in the catalogue with the provision of search from as many segments and angles as possible. This is done in order to provide a wide range of access points to a user or a library staff whosoever intends to refer to a particular document. Cataloguing requires creation of a database.

A database is a collection of files of data of interest to a given library. For each document in a library, a record is maintained which contains descriptive data of sufficient specificity to characterize the document so that from the patrons point of view the existence of the document as well as its location in the library may he determined. The database can be created by using a readily available software package or by writing software by the user agency. This depends upon the financial resources and the local needs of the libraries.

A format is a must for any sort of computerization process. In a computer the need for precision in determining the beginning and the end of every data element needs assignment of codes that can indicate to the computer what kind of element or a part of it is and how much space it occupies. Apart from the data elements, the format consists of fields, which combined together make a record and thus a collection of records is called a database.

Circulation is concerned with the supply of the library materials to the users, to receive it back in the library and also to maintain statistics related with the use. There are only two files required to he maintained for the system; borrower's and item's file. All relevant details about the borrowers and the documents are mounted on the computer and are modified while issuing or returning the document. This is done by a device called the barcoding device. Brocades arc placed on all documents as well as on the Identity Cards of the users and a barcode reader is placed on the circulation desk. The particulars regarding the document and the borrower are downloaded and sent to the Central Processing Unit of the computer where the record is kept in the electronic form. The record is updated at the time. of return of the document. However, some information is retained as it is useful for preparation of utilization report and other related activities.

Details about a particular document are noted down on a data input sheet and then transferred onto computer. The provision of search is incorporated keeping in view the total number of fields in a database, the requirements of the user community and the in-house needs of a library. The computer manipulates the available data depending up on the total number of fields in a database. The details are extracted and fed to meet the short term as well as the long term requirements. It is not always necessary to incorporate a provision of search for each and every field covered up in the database as some of the details are needed very rarely. The following data fields are necessary for computerization of a media library.

Sheet No.		
Title		
Accession No.		Accession Date
Session	Production Year	Telecast Date
Duration	Starts	Ends
Subject		Class No.
Series		Episode
Producer/Director		
Subject Expert/Presenter		
Producing Agency		Place
Produced For		Source
Bill No.	Bill Date	Price
Form		Format
System		Library Tape No.
Generation		
Keyword		
Theme		
Remark's		

In an online information retrieval system, users are supposed to interact with the computer system and find out answers to the problems themselves. A general menu or the summary of holdings is displayed on the visual display unit of the computer out of which the most relevant point is selected and entered for the retrieval of answers. Generally, after pressing a few keys as directed by the computer itself, a researcher is able to retrieve the desired information. In a library attached to a film and television production unit the details frequently required by the users as well as the library staff include production year, telecast date, title, subject class number, producer, duration, library tape number and the synopsis.

Reports may also be generated to cater to the specific needs of the users or of the library staff. For users, a list of title, duration and cassette number can be sufficient to find out a particular programme in case the collection of a media library is not very large. On the other hand, the library staff may need information in many sequences for the in-house activities. However some reports may be needed very rarely like a list of holdings arranged in order of the library tape numbers which may be needed once or twice a year for the purpose of stock verification or to determine the sequence of videocassettes on the library shelves. This will also help in determining as to how many programmes are recorded on an individual cassette.

Information system may be designed for media libraries at micro level too. In a film and television production library a particular stock shot or a sound effect can he of great significance. It may not be easy to reproduce such shots. In a situation like this a 'library shot' is the best answer. An appropriate system of information for the archive shots can reduce the cost of production miraculously. For this, a separate module within the system can he designed. The data input sheet for such documents may include the accession information, title, duration, cassette number, keywords and synopsis.

SYSTEM FOR STOCK SHOTS

Media libraries support in the production process at different stages of production with varied types of library materials. They provide ideas on the topics of programme through subscriptions to periodicals or the press-clipping services. The idea can be further elaborated with the help of books, films and periodicals. The topic of production is usually finalized keeping in view the financial capability, availability of subject experts and the feasibility of shooting. But what we do not take into consideration is the amount of feedback already available in the libraries in the form of stock-shots.

Normally, every producing agency possesses some programmes which might be its own productions or the materials procured from outside. Basically, all the productions must contain reusable shots which can be indexed for their possible use in forthcoming productions.

The production agencies can comfortably use the shots since being their own productions copyright is not a problem for them. The shots from other agencies' productions can be used up to certain duration free of charges. The international Film and Television Archives Association has recommended and restricted the use of shots up to 30 seconds. One particular shot can be used in a number of programmes and in different perspectives, thus conveying different meanings. 'Stock-shot' literally means a shot from the library collection. They are visuals or a combination of audio and vision already available in the library. They can be identified from slide/tape programmes, films or videos. Some of the stock-shots have been used in innumerable productions. The reuse value is directly proportional to their archive value. The live coverage of dropping the atom bomb at Hiroshima and Nagasaki, man's landing on the moon and various expeditions undertaken by mankind have a high archive value. But there arc some stock-shots which saved mankind from a possible disasters too or rather by seeing the impact of these bombs (SCUD 'missiles, etc.) could be a deterrent in future. It could even advocate in preventing the production of these weapons for all times to come. This would depend on how effectively these events arc originally recorded and preserved.

Some shots are very effective. On October 23, 1984 a stock-shot about a drought in Ethiopia was shown by BBC in England and by NBC in the United States of America. Starving children with bloated bellies and stick-like arms in refuge camps were depicted. The effects of this television coverage were immediate and dramatic in the form of a public outpouring of contributions and demands for action. Rock musicians in England and America, previously noted for their over blown egos and free-wheeling lifestyles, altruistically, raised millions of dollars for Ethiopian food relief by holding concerts and by recording songs. The US government also donated funds and soon tanker ships loaded with food grains were docking daily at Ethiopian seaports. A single stock-shot brought into focus the Ethiopian drought problem on the world agenda and saved millions of lives as lost in an early drought.

Stock-shots can be divided into the following four categories:

1 Recordings of Historical Events

2 News Stories

3 Complete Productions

4 Rough Cuts.

Historical events may include visits of dignitaries, launching of new programmes, seminars, international meets and even the events, which seem to be common today but may obtain significance in the time to come. In West Bengal, the government has decided to withdraw the tram service from the city of Kolkata. This might be overlooked being an ordinary event day but is fact significant for a person having futuristic outlook. In the time to come shots on trams will certainly be needed by anyone who attempts to write the history of Kolkata or of the modes of transportation. It will always be better to fulfill the arising requirement in advance. Gandhi and Nehru are no more with us but they are still needed to inspire the generations.

News Stories

New stories are usually available on video or in 16 mm film with combined or separate magnetic sound tracks. They form a valuable source of material for reuse not only for strictly news purposes but also provide a wider range of themes, which can be incorporated for teaching and learning purposes. In fact, every significant event is news at first which goes down slowly into the ages of history. The reusability of the coverage depends upon its news values and also its non-availability. There are news stories, which can never loose their value at any point of time. Even if there are no financial constraints involved in special shooting, the producers may come across difficulties leading to delay in programme production; one cannot wait for the whole year to cover a shot of heavy rain or snowfall. Just imagine waiting a full day to shoot rising sun which may disappoint further if covered with clouds the time of sun rising. In a case like this, the stock-shot is the best answer.

Complete Productions

Stock-shots can be identified from complete film and television programmes available in a library or a group of libraries for resource sharing purposes. Producers use shots from their early productions or from the current productions of others they preview but such use is generally based on the personal memory of the producers or their diaries if maintained by them properly. A computerized information retrieval system can provide an easy access to a vast amount of audio-visual resources. This is slowly becoming inevitable.

Rough Cuts

Shooting is to be done as extensively as possible to provide a wide range of choice to the producers at the time of editing. Normally, the quality of a programme depends upon the ratio of the shot footage and the footage finally retained. In this process most of the coverage is left unused in the form of rough cuts. This may be as great as 40 times of the master production. In New Delhi, a video newsmagazine adds about 40 cassettes a month to their collection even though they produce only a 90 minute programme. They have used their stock-shots repeatedly in a number of issues and show a few shots for business promotion while advertising for the subscription of their video magazine.

INFORMATION SYSTEM

The, characteristics of a computerized information retrieval system and the advantages of such system are as follows;

(a) A common means of access to the library materials.

(b) Accurate, and timely updation of the database.

(c) Continued viability of access to database over a time.

(d) Accurate and timely processing of the new arrivals for availability of all the users.

(e) Recording of and access to status and other information about catalogue transactions.

(f) Strong organization towards patron service and effective access to library materials.

(g) Operation and maintenance of both a dynamically organized and arranged catalogue and collection.

(h) Ability of all units of a library or library system to act in a connected fashion and to have access to all composite lot of data file.

(i) Providing of accurate and reliable statistical data in the form of reporting, management and budget.

(j) Reduction in staff time devoted to those aspects of cataloguing not directly related to users.

In India, the majority of media libraries faces the problem of shortage of staff. They find it difficult even t0 maintain the normal functions of procurement, processing and circulation of the library materials. One can't think of previewing, analysing and indexing individual stock-shots with the existing manpower at the number of individual shots might be hundred time larger comparing the total collection of an audio-visual library.

The Documentation Unit of the TV News Library of Doordarshan in collaboration with the Indian National Scientific Documentation Centre (INSDOC) developed a system for listing of stock-shots having archive value. About 350 different subjects were covered and three separate fills maintained for the retrieval purposes under Tape, Programme and Description or Subject Retrieval. The system was designed for produces and news editors as the target users.

Attempts have also been made for computerizing management of stock shots. The Mass Communication Research Centre of Jamia Millia Islamia in New Delhi was established in 1983. The Centre runs a two year postgraduation course in mass communication and also offers Ph.D. programmes. The second important function of the Centre is the production of the instructional and enrichment materials on sound tapes, colour slides, videotapes or films. The Centre has a Library Resource and Documentation Unit containing collections of books, journals, pressclippings, scripts, 16mm films, audio cassettes, videocassettes and music tapes. Most of the programmes available on video are the productions of the Centre and are recorded on U-Matic cassettes, a format, suitable for broadcast purposes as well as for the purpose of transfer and reuse.

Once the decision to use computer in the Library Resource and Documentation Unit was taken in 1987, the search for a suitable computer software was on. At the same time, UNESCO's package CDS/1SIS was being distributed through the Department of Science and Technology, Government of India. The package was primarily designed to cater to the needs of the libraries, documentation centres and archives. The idea was to cover as many functions of the library as possible. It was found that the version available had not incorporated the required provision whereas being a special library its needs were special. CDS/ISIS was found more suitable for processing of the micro-documents. Being users friendly, it is easier to search through it. Keeping in view the difficulties and limitations, it was decide to develop a software package suitable to the local needs. A system operative on PCs under DOS environment was developed. The main components of the software designed are as follows:

Data Structure

Field	*Type*	*Digital*	*Decimal*
Acc. No.	Numeric	7	–
Acc. Date	Date	8	–
Title	Character	40	–
Start	Numeric	5	2
End	Numeric	5	2
Duration	Numeric	5	2
Cassette No.	Character	10	–
Annotation	Character	200	–
Keywords :			
(1)	Character	20	–
(2)	Character	20	–
(3)	Character	20	–
(4)	Character	20	–
(5)	Character	20	–
(6)	Character	20	–

The software is menu driven and user friendly. It provides the following three options for search:

Keyword Search

One can have access to the desired information entering any of the keywords. For standardization, the keywords are assigned using the *Sears List of Subject Headings.* A dictionary of standard terms is being maintained.

Global Search

Search can be carried out through any of the words appearing in title, keyword or synopsis.

Search Through Cassette/Film Number

This type of search is particularly useful when intended to know about the shots contained in a particular cassette/film.

9

NETWORKING AND RESOURCE SHARING

Almost every country in the world has realized the potential of educational media. In India the most dramatic impact of the Indian National Satellite (INSAT) has been the rapid expansion of television dissemination through installation of more than 750 TV transmitters providing access to over 85% of its population. The use of INSAT for educational broadcasting with about 100 hours of programmes per month to about 4000 schools and colleges has been further augmented.

China use the satellite medium to provide adult educational programmes to 30 million people with 63,000 TVRO earth stations and over 50,000 learning centres. In advanced countries, there is more emphasis on use of this medium for education. They are well equipped with the hardware and the software facilities. The invention of video has reduced the expenditure on production to a great extent. Still it is very costly and needs thorough thinking on the topic and its application before undertaking the work of production. What is needed now is a common database of all such production agencies right from the local to the international level so that it is possible to know what is already available. The efforts to produce such databases and to link them internationally are being made by various organizations.

India has a well knit system of education but the steady growth in its population *is* a problem specially in educating the masses. The dream of 100% literacy rate could not be fulfilled.

In higher education too, we are able to extend the facilities only to about 10% of the total population although there are about 300 universities and 8800 colleges in the country. Educating the masses will be out of reach with the existing traditional system of education based on conventional classroom instruction . The open universities have come up all over the world with the objective of educating the masses. They use distance education mode with a multimedia approach. Now, time and place are no barriers in learning.

In India, the Indira Gandhi National Open University (IGNOU registered a steady growth within a decade of its Inception. The success of IGNOU mainly depended upon the richness of its instructional materials that are available in print as well as in the non-print media. The educational programmes are telecast nationally and are accessible to over 85% of the total population of the country through about 40 million TV receiving sets. The University has also equipped its various study centres spread all over the country to make these programmes accessible to the students. Similarly. the radio programmes are broadcast all over the country. For school education the work of production and telecast has been undertaken by the Central Institute of Educational Technology.

The superiority of the audiovisual method over the existing system of classroom based instruction mainly depends upon the quality of the camera in depicting and presenting objects and events in a way that is quite difficult and almost impossible for a teacher because of several physical limitations. An object can be shown — enlarged or reduced — on screen and the events can be recorded from long distances and also under circumstances where it is not possible for any living being to survive and carry out any activity.

A computer linked with a television and communication link can do wonders. It can retrieve information from anywhere in the world and make it available in any form. The recent advancements in multimedia mail and multimedia document delivery system have international application which can also be adopted for education at all stages.

Most of the universities in the West have made database search an integral part of their studies. Virtually, no research is possible there without consulting the relevant databases. The information networks have sidelined the traditional 'gurus' as far as the selection of the topic of research and the availability of the required amount of materials on the topics are concerned. One can visualize the results of his own efforts in advance because of the availability of the sufficient information on the national as well as the international network,. But it is more applicable in case of the print media.

The use of information and educational technologies primarily depends upon some hardware. The most important among them are the telephone, computer and television. The information is generally imported through the telephone and brought to computer for search, retrieval and downloading. The television is helpful in displaying the audiovisual media. With the operation of Internet, the individual computer linked television sets can work as a channel, permitting not only the preview and downloading of the audiovisual programmes but also for uploading them for their wider use by the others. This will surely permit an unprecedented increase in the quantum of the information available in the audio-visuals.

The prerequisites for computerization, networking and resource sharing are the hardware, the software and the data drawn from all over the country and abroad. The hardware is no more a problem with the advancement in computers, telecommunication technology and the ever increasing .application of satellite in transmission of the audiovisual data. The cost of the hardware is falling considerably and it has come well within the reach of the majority of organisations. A software package may be chosen from amongst the existing ones but may have to be modified suitably as per the needs.

Efforts have been made and are being made to evolve a common communication format for entry of the data regarding the audiovisual programmes by some individual organizations. government and non-government agencies at the national as well as the international levels. The Commonwealth of Learning has established the Commonwealth Educational Media Centre for Asia (CEMCA) which apart from the other media related activities is also involved in standardization of format for data entry and retrieval. The Asian Mass Communication Research and Information Centre in Singapore has also made noticeable efforts in this direction.

The Development and Educational Communication Unit (DECU) of Space Application Centre, Ahmedabad organized a series of workshops to evolve a computerized system suitable to the needs of the media libraries. Similarly the efforts of the Mass Communication Research Centre (MCRC) were also aimed at computerization of their Media Library. There were similarities in the software which were locally developed to meet the demands but they varied slightly. This is merely a reflection of the nature of the educational productions being undertaken by the two organizations. The former is more in the transmission mode whereas the latter's productions are purely educational in nature.

The software package developed by DECU has been improved over the years. The work of improvement was undertaken as a Project of the University Grants Commission for the Consortium for Educational Communication. Accordingly, a series of workshops was organized by DECU which was attended by the representatives of various media organizations in India. Provisions were incorporated in the software keeping in view the requirements Now, it is a user-friendly, menu driven and stand alone package. It is very much in demand in India and abroad. The international agencies like AMIC. Singapore and CEMCA of the Commonwealth of Learning have shown keen interest in the package.

There is an increasing awareness about the need for listing

all the educational television programmes centrally by collecting information from all possible corners of the world. The efforts of various nations are being coordinated in order to achieve the goal of global networking. Individual organizations have joined hands in this exciting venture. In India the common databases for the schools and university level programmes are being developed at the Central Institute of Educational Technology (CIET) and the Consortium for Educational Communication (CEC) respectively. The former collects information from all the State Institutes of Educational Technology and the District Institutes of Education and Training whereas the latter enlists the details of all the productions being undertaken by the Educational Media Research Centres, Audio Visual Research Centers and the similar institutions involved in production of programme for higher education. Still there is no consolidation of these efforts from any single governmental agency to enlist all of them centrally. However, some private distributors have come up with the comprehensive lists of holding which they offer to the buyers.

The Government of India has developed the Education and Research Network (ERNET) with assistance from the United Nations Development Programme in the country. through the Department of Electronics with the initial participation of all the IITs, IISc Bangalore and NCST Bombay, It, represents the most cooperative computer network for the academic and research community. The future areas of the work of Education and Research Network include multi-media mail and multimedia document retrieval in line with the similar efforts in the advanced countries. The Commonwealth of Learning has established CEMCA with the aim of creating a common database for various government and non-government organizations/ institutions in India involved in the dissemination of the multi-media resources. The intention is to facilitate networking of media agencies at a later stage.

A workshop of media librarians drawn from all over the country was organized in the Indira Gandhi National Open University in July, 1995. The Workshop emphasized the importance of creating a common database which would enable cataloging and networking. The format of the workshop was participatory in nature. The importance of a media librarian as an information specialist was emphasized. It was decided to have a common software package for listing of all the productions and resource sharing.

The ultimate aim of CEMCA is to promote cooperation and collaboration among educational and broadcasting organizations in the Commonwealth in the use of electronic media by promoting the development of human resources through the application of distance education techniques and technologies in response to the development needs of the member countries. The deployment of modern communication and information technologies can be a major instrument for widening access to learning, enhancing the quality of education and providing cost-effective education to a large segment of the population for their social and economic betterment. The creation of a common database on educational media resources is the major function of CEMCA.

The Commonwealth of Learning (COL) organized an international conference—'Educational Technology 2000: A Global Vision' for Open and Distance Education which attracted delegates from all over the World who are leaders in distance education and educational technology The Conference received endorsement from several international organizations including UNESCO, SEAMEO, ICDE, CPSE, AAOU and Commonwealth Secretariat. It is the first major attempt in providing an International forum for dialogue between the educational community and the technology industry. The Conference programme was designed to highlight the various sectors of education and the major categories of technologies being employed in education. Now, thanks to the services being provided by the Internet and its range all over the globe. Internet has made it a reality to transmit sound and pictures and facilitate their selection and retrieval easier. In the near future, we will certainly witness an unprecedented growth in the bulk of the audiovisual media resources. The distance learners will be able to retrieve them anywhere in the world. Video and audio signals can be sent round the globe by broadcasting on Internet. Each individual's Internet connection can virtually be used manifold. An individual cannot only receive what is available internationally but can contribute to the resources whatever he or she wishes to upload for the benefit of the mankind. This will facilitate an exponential growth in the bulk of the media resources, consequently, standardisation of methods of entry and retrieval will become mandatory. We have already achieved success in case of the textual information in this direction The Common Communication Format recommended by UNESCO for data entry and retrieval will certainly lead to serious thinking in the matter and the efforts in listing all the available educational media resources drawn from all over the world will soon become a reality for the common man.

The Educational Television (ETV) has grown faster during the last one decade. The setting up of the Mass Communication Research Centre (MCRC) at the Jamia Millia Islamia in New Delhi in 1985 with the assistance of the Canadian International Development Agency is regarded as a milestone in the history of ETV in India. The year is significant because two other national agencies namely the Central Institute of Educational Technology (CIET) and the Indira Gandhi National Open University (IGNOU) were also established in the same year.

India has two well established networks for the ETV production and distribution. The Countrywide Classroom (CWCR) of the University Grants Commission had its modest beginning as INSAT TV Project at MCRC and the first programme under the project went on air on 15th of August 1984. Initially the programmes were aimed at the postgraduate students as sufficient infrastructure was not available to cope with the production needs for the undergraduates. Gratified with the success of the project, the Government of India decided to establish media centres in all the regions of the country. As a result, the Educational Media Research Centres (EMRCs) and the Audio Visual Research Centres (AVRCs) were established. The programmes produced by all these agencies are being telecast by the Consortium for Educational Communication (CEC) in the Countrywide Classroom.

The National Council of Educational Research and Training (NCERT) through CIET caters to the educational needs of the rural primary schools and their teachers. CIET has a network of State Institutes of Educational Technology (SIETs) and the District Institutes of Educational Technology (DIETs). Both CIET and SIETs undertake ETV productions whereas the DIETs only use them for training. Another major ETV producing agency in the country is IGNOU having a network of study centres throughout the country but the work of production is undertaken centrally in its Communications Division. Most of the IITs, IIMs, agricultural universities and government departments have their own infrastructure or hire the services of the private agencies in the trade to produce training programmes for the students and staff aimed at their specific requirements.

In 1984 hardly 20% home-made programmes were telecast in the CWCR and the dependence on the foreign countries mainly USA, Russia, England, Germany and Australia was 80%. Within a decade the Consortium for Educational Communication has created a sound base of around 3,500 programmes excluding the non-broadcast titles. There is another significant change as far as the viewership is concerned. The decision to telecast CWCR programmes in Hindi will yield better results as till today the majority of college and university students in north India do not properly understand the programmes in English.

MCRC again played a lead role in identifying, defining, analysing and mounting on computer the contents of the stock footage collected by way of the rough cuts and extracted from the complete video productions. Along with the information system for books and video a module on management of information available in stock footage was integrated in the multi-media software. The software covers only seven fields i.e. record no. tentative title, subject, duration, position, keyword and synopsis. The provision of global search facilitates retrieval through any of the terms known to the users relating the desired shots.

The Development and Educational Communication Unit (DECU) of the Indian Space Research Organization (ISRO), Ahmedabad has come out with a software package for automation and networking of the libraries of CWCR. Their software has been improved over the years by incorporating changes as a result of the practical difficulties in its use as experienced by the various media centres of CWCR. The software has already been distributed to all the EMRCs and AVRCs with a suggestion to mount the record of productions in the prescribed format. The staff of media centres has been trained in advance for its use. It is possible to improve the software further in order to use it for networking of all CWCR libraries providing the E-Mail facility with the Consortium for Educational Communication as a central agency but despite all the abovementioned efforts the software is not being used by any media centre except MCRC so far.

Networking and resource sharing is possible only after the availability of data, a suitable software package and also the telecommunication link to transmit the information both in the form of text as well as audio visual media in case of the ETV libraries. So far there has not been a single notable effort in centrally listing all the available ETV productions so that a comprehensive record may be available. The first major attempt in compilation of the union catalogue was made by the Electronic Trade and Technology Ltd., New Delhi. They had been basically a supplier of electronic hardware items who occasionally undertook the production as well as the distribution of ETV programmes.

Now the work of distribution has been undertaken by Educational Aid International, New Delhi. In addition to the programmes of CWCR, CIET, SIETs, they cover IITs, IIMs, IGNOU and many other producing agencies for distribution of their ETV productions. MIS Wiley Eastern Limited (WEL) have also become active to supply of educational media. The advantage attached with WEL is that they have a long history of book supply and understand the educational needs of the academic community. Perhaps this is the reason why the sale of their programmes has increased enormously.

Resource sharing among ETV libraries will be useful in many respects. It will not only make possible the compilation of a union catalogue of all the media centres but will also facilitate the finalization of the topics of the forthcoming productions. By sharing the stock shots, which are very rare some times, the cost of production can be minimized considerably. There are instances when the complete video productions have been raised by using the stock footage only and without even touching a camera. Since many of the educational disciplines are closely related and contain the same fragments of subjects it will be possible to use such common shots in all the related programmes.

The telecommunication technology has provided us with the facility of hooking up all the media centres like many other organizations. It allows communication as well as interaction. Two successful attempts can be cited as examples in this context. The National Talkback Experiment of the University Grants Commission conducted came out with the findings that the whole country can be integrated in the form of a classroom. Learners sitting anywhere in the country can interact with the teachers sitting near the earth station. In May 1993 CIET chalked up an interactive teaching experiment on television called Classroom 2000 plus. Students in Hyderabad, Madras and Calcutta were not only able to access the lectures originating from Delhi but also question through telephone links. There have been other successful attempts too like IGNOU/ ISRO Project on video conferencing.

10

Organizational Needs of Media Libraries

The general principles of libraries are common- i.e. collection, preservation and dissemination of information. The library science exists to lay down principles of good practice, which can be applied to all media requiring collection and organization to enhance their usefulness. The audio visual materials can also be catalogued, classified and indexed using the principles and practice of the library science codes and systems, by which standardization can be achieved and local variation of a particular library can be solved with rational approach.

In media libraries, after acquiring a document, a system of cataloguing, classification and indexing has to be adopted, so that the user is able to retrieve relevant information with accuracy and speed. The method to be used should depend very largely on the optimum size of the collection. Obviously, the larger the collection, the greater is the need for laying down principles in respect of acquisition, classification, cataloguing, circulation and finally its use by the academic community in case of the educational media libraries. The term academic community not only includes students but also the teachers and even teachers of teachers.

It has been found in the survey that the component of educational media specially, audiovisual aids increased in greater proportion during the decades of 1970's and 80's. The rate has now been accelerated further with the application of computer and Internet for storage and retrieval of information available in any media formats. It is evident now that the educational media will continue to be used in greater proportion for the instruction and education of human being in the time to come. Therefore, a suitable policy for their development is needed for better results.

Media libraries should be provided adequate space for housing collections and for use of the materials. Any renovation of media space should consider the readily evolving world of digital media and the other requirements of the media libraries.

Libraries having greater proportion of media components have comparatively smaller reading space unlike their print based counterparts. This reflects that the media collections need lesser space for study. Very few libraries possess special type of furniture to shelve the media collections.

Recommended storage and handling practices vary by type of material and by intended use. Access collections should be treated differently from archival collections. Libraries should have policies for all the variations in their particular collection.

The collections of educational libraries require specialized storage and handling. The library should be provided aluminum or wooden racks as the same have no magnetic properties and the materials stored on them will last for more time as compared with the steel racks, which are being generally used in the libraries now a days. While most media resources collections are access collections, some may require more long-term environmental considerations. In such cases, the following measures are required to be taken:

* Store area should be very clean otherwise minute dust particles may cause dropouts (signal lose, short flashes in the picture etc.)

* Air conditioned room/space with the facility of controlling temperature and humidity as recommended by tape manufacturers may be provided for video and audio tapes.
* Metallic iron stacks open from both sides may be provided for storing/keeping video/audio cassettes/tapes.
* Tapes should be handled with extreme care.
* Always check tapes and keep with proper winding.
* Periodic rewinding of tapes is necessary for ventilation purpose. This may be done atleast once a year if they have not been used for along period.
* Master copy of video/audio should be stored/stacked separately from duplicate copy.
* Tapes should be kept vertically on the shelves.
* Fire extinguishers must be provided in the stores.
* Tape Librarian should be aware about the common tape problems.

Media equipment is essential to providing access to media resources. The library should establish an ample and stable budget for the maintenance and purchase of media equipment. The addition and replacement of equipment should be based upon a written plan. Libraries cannot provide access to media resources without sufficient and well-maintained equipment. The level of funding should be based upon the life expectancy for equipment and in-house use of the collection. A budget plan for media equipment should include the repair and replacement of worn equipment, the need to provide upgrades to existing equipment, and the purchase of additional equipment as user demand increases.

The plan should also anticipate the adoption of new technologies and the need to expand support for new kinds of equipment. Equipment maintenance and replacement have a major impact on the longevity of collections.

Personnel requirements for maintaining media libraries involve a variety of skills The collection requires maintenance. In smaller libraries only one person may have ail the responsibilities of maintenance, while in larger libraries, persons may be hired to perform specific tasks therefore, the librarian must be cognizant to maintenance needs of the various types of media.

Proper staffing of the libraries is also a must to achieve goals of the organization. The person responsible for the media library should have at least a post-graduate degree in library and information science

The library staff with other media-related degrees may bring expertise to a library but the service will be strengthened if managed by a qualified librarian. This librarian should have qualified or experienced in working with academic library media resources. This may include film studies, mass communications, computer. Internet application in libraries- multimedia or related fields, depending upon the scope of the librarian's responsibilities.

The media librarian should take a proactive role within the institution, beyond the library, working cooperatively and collaboratively with personnel in other media-related units on campus. Most colleges and universities have more than one unit delivering media services. The media librarian should actively promote the library's collections and services among these personnel and plan cooperative ventures with them as appropriate.

Information has become the biggest instrument for the progress of mankind. Various countries have already proceeded on this path. India, in its unique way has taken up the route. The generation, exchange and utilization of information requires that the information and library science personnel in India of the present and future are duly equipped with the role of information consultants and managers. This idea should be applicable to every field of library and information profession and is much needed for the growing media related disciplines.

The new situation has obviously called for drastic changes in the training of media librarians, and to be sure the best library schools have been modifying curricula to keep abreast of evolving needs.

Library schools should evolve special training programmes and academic courses for management of such libraries. Moreover, media librarians should be encouraged to belong to and participate in media-related professional associations and other professional development activities.

The Curriculum Development Committee of UGC has suggested various courses to be organized for the librarians keeping in view the present needs of the profession including Music Librarianship, Non Book Material and Media Librarianship and AV Library materials. It has also suggested a course at post graduation level, which is entitled Communication, Mass Media and Public Library for the one year master degrees programme of M. Lib. I. Sc, as an optional subject. But in view of the rapid development of educational media and the problems of its management for educational purposes, a course on Educational Media Librarianship may also be introduced. It can be an optional course for the students at the graduation as well as post graduation level. Alternately, the course may be conducted as:

(a) Refresher course

(b) Summer course

(c) Winter course

(d) Short term course

Short term courses may be organized through IASLIC, ILA, DRTC, INSDOC, DESIDOC, NIC, NISSAT and many other media organizations such as Consortium for Educational Communication, Development and Educational Communication, Indian Space Research Organization, Ahmedabad, radio, film and television organizations etc.

It is likely that the media librarian will be the only professional within the library working predominantly with media resources. Because of the issues inherent to collecting and delivering media resources, other media librarians are often the only source of professional support and specialized information. Organizations should fund continuing education opportunities and conference attendance for the librarian responsible for the media program.

The changing nature of media resources and ongoing changes in technology may exceed the expectations for all library staff. Most academic libraries have only one media librarian; thus, conferences afford important opportunities to share ideas with other media librarians and attend relevant meetings. Such facilities should be provided to the media librarians as they are already applicable in case of the other library professionals working in the academic environment.

Budget is the primary means by which formulated plans are carried out. It is the most important control device to measure programme of a library and its effectiveness. Thus budget is crucial for the success of a library towards meeting the needs of its users.

The four essentials of good budgeting are effective organization, administrative support, effective accounting and research. Good organization provides the structure within which to plan and carry out fiscal programmes. All academic libraries should provide adequate funding for media services and collections; "adequate funding" is determined by the library's goals and objectives for media services and collections. ACRL standards provide evaluative measures for the adequacy of the budget. These measures should be applied to funding for media collections and services.

An ample and stable budget for the acquisition of media resources should be based either on a percentage of the total library acquisitions budget or on a formula related to collection use as measured by circulation statistics. Basing the media resources materials budget on a percentage of the acquisitions budget assures that large academic libraries allocate a reasonable amount of funding to building media resources collections. Using circulation statistics to determine funding levels for the purchase of media resources assures that a high-use collection will be able to meet the demand for new titles, additional copies of popular titles, and replacement of worn materials. Materials budgets should also be large and flexible enough to support the exploration of new media formats along with traditional format

The major goal of acquisition is to procure the resources that are needed to achieve the library's objective. The function includes selection, ordering and payment for the materials purchased.

No common and popular specifications have been derived for acquisition of the media materials as compared with its print counterpart. But there are certain pre-cautions to be observed while adding the collection of media to the libraries like clarification of terms and conditions regarding the purchase and rights to use the materials.

The library should have a separate, written collection development policy statement to serve as the basis for selection and acquisition of media resources. The library's overall collection development policy should include media resources, but a separate policy is needed to establish priorities and guide selections. Selection decisions are different from format to format. These differences must be described in the collection development and selection policies.

The selection of media resources materials should be the shared responsibility of librarians specifically charged with building the media resources collection and the subject selectors. The selection of media resources is different from the selection of print materials. Media selection requires the use of specialized review sources and may include previewing of materials under consideration or purchasing on approval. Media selectors need special training and skills. However, subject selectors provide necessary content expertise when considering more specialized media resources. The media resources reference collection should include a wide selection of standard works and specialized reference tools in all formats. Obsolete and worn out materials should be systematically removed from the collection and replaced if necessary. Worn materials represent a hazard to equipment. Most academic libraries, including research libraries, do not maintain archival media collections on site, due to the need to maintain outdated equipment. These materials are usually housed in separate archival collections.

As equipment becomes obsolete and unavailable, the media librarian should have a plan for preserving, the content of the software- The procedures for decision making should consider whether the materials are in an archival collection or in an access collection and whether they should be replaced or reformatted. Permission to reformat may need to be secured from the copyright holder. However, the 1998 Digital Millennium Copyright Act permits the reformatting of materials from obsolete formats without permission.

Library materials are meant for use. They need proper organization so that the user with or without the knowledge of library organization is able to find the desired library materials. There are probably as many ways of organizing the documents as there are media libraries. In a particular library emphasis can be on one or two types of materials while there may be general collections of many kinds of non- book materials. The various procedures such as cataloguing, classification, key words, subject headings etc.which help in finding the relevant information in all type of libraries.

Media resources should be catalogued in a timely fashion, with a sufficient level of support for cataloguers, equipment, and training to ensure that the materials will not be backlogged. Media resources generally require more complex cataloging routines and lengthier bibliographic descriptions. They also have physical characteristics that require unique processing. Therefore, media resources take more time to catalog and process than most print resources. Trained professional cataloguers with media expertise require access to appropriate cataloguing and indexing tools, playback equipment in all formats represented in the collection, and the Web.

The responsibilities and functions of the media libraries should be clearly defined within the organizational structure of the library. The administration of the library should assign responsibility for the media library to a librarian. In order to develop an effective media resources program, a librarian must be responsible for planning collections and services. Depending upon the organizational structure of the library, this librarian should manage a separate media resources unit or department, which may work within another library unit, or coordinate the activities of librarians (for example, subject specialists) and other staff from several units, computing center personnel particularly those involved with multimedia.

Media materials should be arranged in libraries in a convenient way. They may be arranged according to the subject content or in accession wise sequence or on APUPA pattern as suggested by Dr. S. R. Ranganathan.

Service is the ultimate goal of a library. Media Libraries should offer assistance to educators who want to integrate the use of media resources into their courses, either as a part of classroom instruction or as supplemental study in the library. The media librarian should actively promote use of the collection in teaching by offering services to faculty in locating local media resources for a new or revised course, suggesting ways in which these materials might be used, locating resources available at other libraries or for purchase and generally assisting in the use of these materials. Media librarians should be included on collaborative teams developing new courses, as many faculty are unfamiliar with the tools needed to locate and evaluate media resources.

Specialized media-related reference services supported by appropriate print and electronic reference sources should be available to assist the students, faculty, and staff in meeting their instructional, informational, and research needs. Users may need assistance in identifying relevant media resources to use in instruction and research. Instructors may need assistance in developing instruction using media resources. General reference librarians often do not have the necessary training to provide these information services.

While most other information sources are designed to be used by individual users, many media libraries are designed to be used in groups. Others are used by individuals. Libraries must accommodate all types of users in a variety of settings

Instruction programs should incorporate the use of media resources as information sources for instruction and research just as instruction programs have now incorporated information available on the Web, locating and using media resources should also be a part of library instruction. Library courses and instruction in information literacy should include visual literacy and media literacy

The necessary equipment to access media resources should be available and maintained to provide ready access to collections. Media collections cannot be used without the necessary playback equipment. While some media collections circulate outside the library. Some users do not own or have access to playback equipment. It must be available in the library not only to facilitate the preview but also attract users.

Technology used in teaching, learning, and research has created new challenges and opportunities for library media resource collections and services. Librarians must also consider computer technology and emerging digital formats. Since development in multimedia and Internet encompass all type of documents this phenomenon is likely to get more and more relevance in the time to come. Media resources should be available in a variety of playback situations, including a mixture of individual, small group, and large group viewing facilities. They should also use the computer technology for better utilization of the resources

The following are the urgent technical needs of the libraries:

(1) Since most of the media librarians use computers on shared basis they should be provided separate computer systems preferably Pentium.

(2) Media libraries may use any software of their choice but the same should have the provision of CCF since it would permit standardization and facilitate resource sharing and networking.

The issues regarding the technical needs of media libraries are of urgent nature since both the technology and media are developing simultaneously. It is therefore suggested to fulfill their technical needs on priority basis in a phased manner as below:

Phase I

1. Availability of Computer hardware.
2. Training of media librarians in use of computers
3. Training of media librarians in technical processing of the materials i.e. cataloguing, classification etc.
4. Availability of preview facility in media libraries
5. Availability of data entry operator in the media libraries.

Phase II

1. Delivery of software packages
2. Training of media librarians on the software package to be used
3. Establishing procedure for networking

Phase III

1. Establishment of networking systems
2. Invite 'persons with expertise in networking to give the requirements and make the plans operational
3. Training in networking.

Databases of holdings of the libraries should be created without any further delay since it would facilitate the compilation of union cataloguing, networking and resource sharing. Consequently, it will promote the use of the library materials that is very much feasible now with the help of Internet.

11

Computer and the University Libraries

Computer has been successfully introduced in many sectors like the airlines, railways, defense and hotel management. Primarily concerned with information, library collection, storage and distribution naturally involve more quantitative exchange of information compared with any other organization. And, that makes the automation of libraries a rather difficult job.

University libraries in India have a glorious past. A glance at the development in the last century shows that they not only grew in number exponentially but also the services being provided by them were recognised internationally. Dr. S.R. Ranganathan made a great contribution to the field and proved that the Indian techniques of dealing with the knowledge and information were not inferior to that of any other country in the world.

Computerization of major academic libraries involves capital investment in terms of human energy, cost and time. It takes years, and not months, to achieve automation in the university libraries because of their complex problems of collection management and staffing even if adequate finances were available. After introducing automation, the switching over from the existing manual system is followed by a process called "parallel run" that is exercised to test the reliability of the new system. It must always be remembered that the manual system is not inferior to the computerised one and the superiority of the latter rests solely with the capacity and efficiency of computer over man. There should be enough room for reverting to the manual system in the event of failure of computerisation in the absence of a proper environment.

A man can take suitable decisions in an environment of confusion but a computer fails at the very start if instructions are not clear. For accuracy in output a computer needs accuracy in its input. It can neither think nor create on its own. Even a minor error in a computerised system is reflected instantly whereas the same can be ignored in a manual system.

Librarians in the universities have a dual responsibility of updating their records according to the requirements of automation and also to maintain uniformity and consistency in the records since most of the university libraries are large and old. While planning to design a system, the international bibliographic standard has also to be taken into consideration.

The university libraries in India registered a steady growth during the last five decades because of the larger amount of funds available to the universities. But not much attention has been paid to standardisation of the information systems among them. We have as many ways of collection management as is their number. Unesco has recommended a Common Communication Format (CCF) to all the libraries and other information agencies for recording of data with the intention of bringing uniformity to recording and retrieval.

As an impact of technology on the profession, some practices in library profession, are losing their significance like classification and cataloguing. The various schemes of classification were promulgated to facilitate the retrieval of documents in view of the limitation of human memory to keep pace with the huge collection of books and also for coordination of concept so that the related subjects may be grouped together. But it is now being substituted by the vast memory, speed and accuracy of computer systems that can retrieve the required segment of information from a huge library collection or online databases. The concepts can be coordinated on the computer screens.

In cataloguing, the entry element was vital to facilitate access. Now, information can be retrieved in any desired sequence. The provisions for search through any field contained in the database can be incorporated in accordance with the necessities of an individual library. The present trend show that the catalogue cards will be replaced or sidelined *soon by* Online Public Access Catalogue (OPAC).

The present university system was designed by the previous generation of librarians in response to the prevailing conditions of that time. The system responded to the situation very well but it needs changes in the present perspective when a number of IT gadgets have emerged during the last one decade. They are affecting the library and information activities and the impact is clearly visible on the university libraries since they are very closely linked with research and development.

Various government agencies like UNESCO, INSDOC, DESIDOC, AICTE, Dept. of Electronics and Planning Commission offer assistance in modernization of university libraries. The University Grants Commission besides making funds available, sanctioned the post of information scientist for every university library for computerisation. Barring a few of them, the progress is far from satisfactory.

The Information and Library Network (INFLIBNET) Project was launched in the eighties with an objective of linking the university and college libraries of the country for the purpose of resource sharing and reduction in the expenditure on books and journals by avoiding purchase of duplicate copies.

Now, the task of computerisation is not so difficult as before. The purchase of suitable hardware could have been a problem ten years ago but it is well within the limit for any institute of higher education now. A document generally needs 500 bytes of information to the most for its processing in libraries and thus a computer with 20 or 40 GB hard disk drive can easily accommodate a large number of documents that only very big libraries might be holding. In case of the software when no understanding could reach on a uniform software package it is optional for the institutions to choose the package of their own choice, which contains the provision of data conversion as per the common communication format.

Computer is now the basis for about all types of modern libraries. It offers them services on cheaper cost comparing with the print media. For instance, the Encyclopedia Britannica is available cheaper on CD ROM than in print and apart from providing all the information as available on paper it facilitates speedy retrieval and connects the users with thousands of sites on Internet as an additional advantage. It is also updated instantly.

Libraries can no longer be viewed as passive and non-profit organisations. Unfortunately, most of the university libraries are not in a position of generating their own revenues. On the one hand the expenses may be minimized by rational expenditure on collection development and drawing benefits from the services offered through the coordinated efforts of the Government while on the other hand, revenues can also be generated in the libraries itself.

The process of privatisation has started in India on the pattern of the advanced countries. University libraries should grab the opportunities in order to survive. Dr. Thompson in his book 'Library Power' says "libraries are institutions charged with the duty of providing the means for the perpetual self education of one and all, and then contribute to the circulation of ideas, the demand of democracy, the spread of literacy and the success of commercial and industrial enterprises". The status of a university is judged by the standard of its library.

University libraries have a tremendous potential to provide

services to business and industrial houses of their areas and to earn money from them. This earning can be used for strengthening of library services at a low cost for the academic world. This can be achieved by properly informing the relevant user groups of the materials available on their demands and their demands can be recorded in the form of the user profiles.

A study conducted by Rebecca Adler (MC Journal: The Journal of Academic Media Librarianship vol. 5 No. 2,1997) indicates that the changes in schools of library and information science curricula are drastic. They have not only changed their curricula but have virtually redefined the field as well. A number of library schools in the United States have changed their names to reflect the information science/studies components of their programmes, and they now offer joint degree programmes with other related departments of their respective institutions, e.g. computer science, communications, telecommunications, cognitive psychology etc.

The process of changing curricula and making more relevant to the technical needs of the libraries has started in India too. Dr. Bhim Rao Ambedkar University at Agra designed and introduced the course Master of Information Management and Technology a few years back. The course is having components of Library Science, Media and Information Technology Similarly, almost all the institutions have changed the names of their departments from Library Science to Library and Information Science and inducted segments of Information Technology in their courses.

In the time to come, the role of librarians will change. Training of users will become a major activity for them since everybody will have enough amount of information within reach and only the retrieval techniques will be needed to obtain it.

User education is imparted to students to explain the techniques of information storage and retrieval so that they could be made self-dependent or less dependent in matters of locating the desired information. The practice continued in the past and still there are some institutions which impart user education. Perhaps there is no university library barring a few agricultural universities where user education is being imparted as part of their regular course.

The university libraries should design courses on user education and impart training to the users specially with reference to use of computer for storage, management and retrieval of information. Library is the most appropriate place for such an activity since it is better equipped with the information retrieval equipment in comparison of any other department of study. Even the departments of library and information studies do not have adequate facilities to demonstrate the practical procedure of retrieval as far as the variety of the information media and the retrieval machinery is concerned.

It is clear now that the future belongs to information technology and the university libraries being the most appropriate organs for transaction of information and creation of new knowledge will heavily depend upon it in the time to come. By adoption of the latest information technology i.e. multimedia. Internet and electronic publishing, they can meet serious challenges from external forces like the enormous explosion of information and knowledge and resource crunch. There should be more emphasis on adoption of the latest gadget and techniques of information storage and retrieval since they are vital for survival of the university libraries. The library staff serving the university libraries also needs training in application of the latest information technology and also better service conditions so that they may continue to play an effective role in future.

COMPUTER APPLICATION

Information systems for libraries are jointly designed by the library and the computer professionals. The former study their requirements and present them in a logical sequence whereas the latter incorporate suitable provisions in the software in order to meet those requirements. Both of them analyze the same functions but their approaches are different. In the larger libraries, they are mediated by systems librarians who have exposure to the knowledge of computer as well as library. It is intended to extract and put on computer the maximum amount of information about documents and incorporate as many options of search and manipulation as possible.

A computer understands instructions in a machine language through a data input device. One document/record is generally represented by one data sheet and a database is a collection of records available to a computer that can be manipulated depending upon the provisions incorporated in the software and also the capability of the hardware. The data is required to be fed only once and stored properly. The economy in storage and the speed of operations for search and retrieval depends upon the efficiency of both the hardware and the software.

The deficiencies in the existing manual systems are of varied nature and can mainly be attributed to improper maintenance of records, lack of updation, periodic gaps and also switching over from one system to the other without establishing any one in full. There are instances when different schemes of classification were followed by one university library but none of them worked for the whole collection. This contributes to confusion and creates an unworkable environment for automation since the clarity and consistency of records is the first and the foremost condition for automation.

Presently, there is no established practice of conducting system rectification in the university libraries. The work is occasionally undertaken by the technical or stock verification sections. But there is a clear distinction between stock verification and system rectification. Stock verification is carried out to determine the loss to the collection by way of theft, damage or non return of documents from users whereas the system rectification aims at updation of the overall records of the libraries.

System rectification can be conducted by updating the existing records of libraries, proper arrangement of documents on shelves and by maintaining a separate cadre of library professionals for the purpose out of the technical wings. It is needed to modify records so as to reflect the current position of documents. A lot of human energy and computer memory can be saved for better ends if only relevant records are mounted. Separate files for the written off and weeded out books can be maintained to avoid confusion and save computer memory since such documents are not available for circulation and their records are rarely consulted. In case of a new library emerging out the existing ones, the records of all the contributing libraries should be modified simultaneously as in the larger academic institutions newer departments of study emerge and the libraries are established to provide them the required academic support.

In the university libraries, the research and reference collections are arranged at many stages. The current publications are kept on the reference desk itself. They are shifted to the stacks whenever their newer issues arrive and remain there for about five years. Ultimately, such collections are sent to their permanent place in the library. As the documents move from one place to the other, the records should also indicate their current position.

The systematic arrangement of documents on shelves is a must for automation. The classification and cataloguing methods can only provide details regarding the place of documents in the collection but the objective of their utility can never be fulfilled in the absence of harmony between the record and the physical position of the document. It is really a time consuming process but without this computerisation and even the manual system fails to work. The university libraries generally follow the open access system in circulation of documents wherein users are allowed to go to shelves directly and take out the required materials themselves. In the process of taking out and shelving, books are normally displaced and such books in a large collection are as good as lost since they are not available for use in the hour of need.

The nature of the job of system rectification warrants creation of a separate cadre of professionals drawn from the hard core of the library profession. There is a clear categorization of work in the university libraries. Two streams of staff can conveniently be identified; the staff performing the administrative jobs is mainly responsible for selection, ordering, payment, circulation, services and the overall supervision of the library whereas the technical or systems staff is entrusted with accessioning, cataloguing and stock verification. Thus the expertise earned through experience in the technical services can be put to a better use in computerisation. There are already three separate cadres in the university administration headed by the registrar, finance officer and controller of examinations and admissions. On these lines, the system cadre can also be drawn from the existing staff in the university libraries.

The manpower engaged in computerisation of libraries has brighter career prospects compared with their other colleagues in the profession. There are more openings for them. It is evident from their frequent shifting from one organization to the other. No longer they can be attracted and satisfied with lip service. The time has come to realize the importance of their role and create a workable environment for them leading to job satisfaction so that the crisis of brain drain is averted from the libraries.

To a few, the solution may lie in employing software experts for automation of the university libraries thus replacing or sidelining librarians. But the past experiences show that no major library can be computerised without the active participation of librarians. Adequate knowledge of the subject and practical experience of managerial level is essential for analyzing functions and suggesting provisions for data entry and operation.

The current advancement in hardware and software of computers, their consistently lowering prices and the enhancement in the quality and capacity of computers have made them affordable and user friendly. The market is full of the readily available packages specially designed for automation of the university libraries. One can find over a dozen such packages, which have successfully been applied and are being used. Still there are many reasons for delay and failure. The most significant among them is the non-availability of the retrospective record in a proper order. The simplicity of the library systems transforms into complexity whenever a library collection grows and becomes decentralized as it is very common in case of the university libraries. Now, the hardware, software and even operation of the system is no problem and only the rectification of records is needed for application of the computer and proper utilization of the library resources.

Computerization of the university libraries is a must for many other reasons too. The cost of publications is escalating at an annual rate of 15% for the scientific and technical literature and somewhere between 10 to 15% in case of the social sciences and the humanities. Secondly, there is the infoımation explosion. As a result, more and more literature is available for the academic institutions. It is very difficult and almost out of reach for the university libraries to update their collections in the present circumstances.

We plan more for the retrieval functions in the name of computerization leaving aside the first and the foremost work of data entry to make it available in the electronic form. Our university libraries must have a definite plan of computerization. For this, ways may be different but the first step should be the initiation of data entry. It simply needs the computer hardware and the software.

It has been observed that even after procurement of hardware and software the work does not start for a long time. This is a very harmful tendency in automation since the expected life of a computer system is about five years. By the time computerization is achieved an entirely new system outdates the existing ones. Then, there arises the problem of maintaining such systems. Most of the maintenance agencies refuse to take annual contracts for the older systems. Alternately, it needs consultancy of high professionals to run the system, which is almost out of reach for the libraries. The time of launching computerization should be fixed up in accordance with the expected availability of hardware software and the data entry staff as most of the problems confront at the initial stage.

In the past, computerization meant involvement of professors, scientists, engineers etc. This tendency still prevails. As a result, many persons are required to coordinate the work. This naturally delays the process. The most unfortunate decision is to allow the technocrats to develop software and ignore the expertise of librarians. Where there is an active involvement of librarians, the rate of computerization is taster such as in case of the libraries of Planning Commission, Parliament House, Indian Institute of Public Administration, IITs and IIMs etc. There is hardly any university in the country now, which can claim such achievements in automation.

Our expectations from computerization are very high at the time of beginning. We usually think of adopting many additional services such as (a) facility to search national and international databases, (b) setting up of the electronic library of CD ROM databases, (c) design and development of Open Public Access Catalogue in machine readable form, and (d) setting up of Desk Top Publishing system. These expectations are hardly realised but the whole process of computerization is delayed because of it.

Computerization of new and smaller libraries is easier compared to the older and the larger ones. But most of the university libraries have emerged from the smaller libraries of the past. They have inherited with them the traditional systems of their maintenance. Computerization is based on the modern and standardized systems, which are rare in the older libraries. Their systems have to be standardized and modified in accordance with the necessity of automation. This is possible by conducting stock and system verification.

In the past, the fear of machines for librarians and the high cost of computers restricted their application in libraries. The fear has been eliminated because of the availability of user friendly and menu driven packages specially developed for automation of libraries. The machines of enhanced quality are available now a days on comparatively lower costs. This has been possible with the advancement in electronics and specially in the microchip technology based on Very Large Scale Integration (VLSI).

The selection of hardware is made keeping in view the quantum of data to be processed and the services expected. A larger university library may have needed a super computer had the automation been planned a decade back. In the changed circumstance of today even a mainframe is regarded as more than sufficient for such a library. Pentium, a personal computer with 40 GB memory that is available with an ordinary computer now-a-days can accommodate the whole bibliographical details of an average university library. Its memory can be extended further if needed as applicable in most of the systems. Some peripheral devices can also be attached with Pentium to divide the additional load and to permit decentralization of functions.

The larger university library systems can be computerized systematically by computerizing all the libraries under the system one after the other. The first phase may cover the automation of the central libraries and the satellite libraries within an university system can be connected with the help of a telecommunication link for the purpose of networking and resource sharing.

The office of the librarian should be the central nodal agency with the most powerful computer system. The databases developed anywhere in the libraries should be available on this system. The major divisions of the central library should be provided terminals or computers as per their needs. Each of the major satellite libraries can also be equipped with an independent system to cope with the load and also to meet future needs.

Software for a major library should be chosen with great care. Basically, there are two options for it. The software can be developed locally and it can also be procured from the market. Experience shows that the locally developed software generally fail after sometimes. This is particularly relevant in case of the university libraries. The main reason being that the software development needs high professional skills and continuous updating even after its application. It is better to opt for the branded packages since they are the only effective substitute now.

The market is full of the readily available packages specially designed for library automation. Some of them have already proved dependable after their application. LIBSYS and LTBRIS are the packages designed to suit the library needs in the Indian context. The provisions for in-house as well as the retrieval functions have been incorporated. Their vendors undertake warranty to train the operating staff and run the system for the desired periods. These software are menu driven and user friendly and need lesser computer skill compared with the CD/ ISIS and many other packages. LIBSYS has been refined over the years. It is operational in DOS, ZENIX and UNIX environment

There is a provision of conversion of data in most of the packages. It means that the data entered into the system using any library software can be made accessible for the other. Unesco has prescribed some basic entry elements for all the software developers in order to standardize formats and permit global resource sharing among the desired institutions. This format is called the Common Communication Format (CCF).

The accession information is the basis for automation. It is extracted from the documents as well as from all other possible sources at the time of procurement. Thus the maximum details gathered are recorded in a standardized format called the accession register, in a computerized system these details are entered once only, stored properly and manipulated in the desired sequences.

The current data can be entered straightaway from the accession records as a routine work. However, additional staff or private agencies can be engaged for entry of the retrospective data. The agencies undertaking data entry have quite varying rates for their work. Sometimes, they quote charges for data collection also.

Computer has proved to be the most powerful tool for management of information. But in the Indian universities its potential has not been realised properly. The university libraries have to face the challenge of computer as the coming generations will depend more on it. Or, this gap in library profession will adversely affect the overall process of education. The purpose of library automation is to free the librarians from the routine clerical work and to allow them to contribute more meaningfully to spread of knowledge and information. In the functioning of libraries, there are many repetitive jobs, which can be easily handled by computer and a lot of human energy thus saved can be put to a better use.

Standardization allows proper sharing of resources among the desiring institutions. For this, processing of all documents of the libraries is required to be undertaken according to the standardization norms. The work is to be taken up both outside the libraries and inside just as the centralized accessioning has become a common feature in most of the university libraries. This saves a lot of expenditure avoiding ordering of duplicate copies, which are not needed and can be shared by other libraries.

DATABASE CREATION

Information systems are designed to facilitate access to a huge amount of data. The system may be manual or computerised. But the computerised systems are advantageous over the manual ones. They reduce the energy and time taken in the repetitive processes of the libraries and reflect their holdings instantly and from various angles of search which is not possible in the traditional systems due to physical limitations.

Designing of information systems for automation of university libraries is a joint venture of librarians and software engineers. The former present their requirement into a logical order and the latter incorporate suitable provision to make the system work. Both of them analyze the same functions but their approaches are different. Now, the work of system designing has become easier with the availability of ready made software packages for automation of the libraries.

University libraries hold documents of varied nature. Moreover, there are many categories of users namely, students, teachers, staff and their subcategories. It needs careful planning to computerise them. A step by step approach is needed for database creation. The first and the foremost requirement is to make available the suitable hardware and software and then convert the bibliographic data into machine readable form.

A database is a set of data that is related to each other. The Microsoft Corporation defines it as "a collection of information that is related to particular subject or purpose". A dictionary or an encyclopaedia being arranged logically and complete in itself may be taken as an example of manual database. The advantages of computerized databases are many over the manual ones on account of the vast memory, speed and accuracy of computer which stores, processes and delivers information once fed into the desired sequences.

The databases created in the university libraries may conveniently be put under two broad categories according to the nature of records they consist i.e. the information regarding documents and users respectively. As almost all the university libraries are still print media based. The databases designed for them are the bibliographical databases.

The futuristic approach for database creation includes imagination and policy making for atleast 10 years in advance. The computer hardware has acquired maturity and the degree of sufficiency that is needed for university libraries, but new experiments are still taking place in the software industry.

There are software which offer management of multimedia and multilingual collections and a also allow remote access not only from the libraries but also to the libraries from one's work place. These options are costly and out of reach generally for an average library but the university libraries being larger enough may go for them for better results. In India, such software are still in the stage of infancy.

Training of staff in maintenance of the hardware and software and also in extraction of the required data from the documents is an essential part of the work of database creation. The hardware and software suppliers undertake to impart the working knowledge about their products but the extraction of data becomes the responsibility of the libraries. Moreover, there may be some local variations in respect of the presentation of the various segments of the database as per the needs of an individual library that is taken care of by the library itself.

The following are the three major sources from where data can be extracted and mounted on computer in order to create a bibliographical database.

The best and the most appropriate source for data entry is the document. Being complete in itself, a document provides the maximum possible details. In some cases the body of the text is also consulted for bringing out the required information that is not available anywhere else. Every library maintains record of documents in a standardised format to facilitate the inventory control. The two broad categories of such records are Accession Registers and Catalogue Cards

All possible details about a particular document are copied in the accession register at the time of purchase. The format of the register is approved by the Government and it is more for administrative exercises rather than for retrieval functions. It does not provide column for subject headings and key words. Moreover, libraries generally do not write class numbers in it although a column has been provided for the same. In view of these limitations, the accession register is generally not used as a source for data entry. But it is of great help when the *other* sources fail to provide details about a particular document.

Every library maintains catalogue cards of different categories like author, title, subject, classified etc. Another category of card maintained behind the scene are shelf cards. They are of utmost value for automation. It is the confidential record of library kept in the high security zone and maintained in a classified order. University libraries generally go for data entry through this record for retrospective conversion.

Various new methods of data entry have emerged with the advancement in the hardware and software. Big libraries in the developed countries purchase pool of bibliographical data and extract records of those documents which are to be added to the library. The catalogue of Library of Congress may be acquired on CD ROMs or online for transfer of the relevant entries to the developing database of the interested libraries. This allows speed and accuracy. Further, the data so entered is available in a standardised forma, which can be shared on national as well as the international level. The bigger the library the more advantageous and economic is this method of data entry.

Libraries normally have to decide a cut off date for automation. All new arrivals are processed in the changed environment after this date. Data entry for such books starts right from the acquisition section, which deals with the selection, ordering and purchase of documents. As per the provisions incorporated in the software packages, the information is required to be entered only once and the same is imported by the other concerned sections of he library to perform a variety of Functions as per their specific needs.

Retrospective data refers to the record of the documents, which have already been purchased and processed in the library before the cut off date. A large amount of data about the existing collections of libraries belongs to this category which is required to be mounted on the systems as a pre requisite to automation. It can generally be achieved in two ways i.e. by entry through books or through catalogue cards. The former is done on a regular basis for the current arrivals whereas the popular practice followed in case of retrospective conversion is the latter.

The most time taking process in computerisation is data entry. It needs the services of professionals trained in extraction of the bibliographical data from the documents and mounting it on a computer. In case of the retrospective data. It is necessary to ensure that only those documents are taken up for the task which are available in the library physically or on record, otherwise not only the precious time of the staff is wasted but also the complications in automation increases which contributes to confusion and inaction. To avoid such a situation, there are certain practices in the libraries and the most effective of them is the rectification of the library collections; both books as well as the shelf record are arranged properly and then compared with each other.

Retrospective conversion of data is the main problem for the university libraries. They generally engage outside agencies for the work. But it largely depends upon the availability of funds. The rates for entry through books are comparatively higher and only a few university libraries are able to meet the expenditure to be incurred in such a case. In the normal circumstances, the rates for data entry through books range from Rs. 7 to 40 per record depending upon the specifications. Since books are the original sources of bibliographical data, entry through books should be preferred if affordable.

University libraries generally invite quotations for data entry indicating their terms and conditions including the details of fields, tags, subject headings, key words etc. to be covered, keeping in view the provision of standardisation of the entered data for resource sharing.

There are some agencies which supply automation software and also undertake data conversion from one format to the other so that the energy consumed in entering data on other software is saved and put to judicious use.

After the data entry in respect of a collection or section of the library is over, the next step should be to compare the entered data with the concerned books. As the physical arrangement of books on shelves is the same for both the manual as well as computerised system, they may easily be compared for reliability. This can be achieved by generating a hard copy of the entered data in a classified order and taking it to the shelves for comparison. It will not only facilitate the perfect arrangement of documents but also make it possible to rectify the stock side by side.

In big libraries, large number of books, which should have been available on the stacks according to the shelf record may not be found at their respective places while comparing with the entered data. The reason for this may be price charge for the lost books, transfer of books from one stock to the other and also the issue without maintaining proper record.

It is also necessary to channelise the issue record during the period of comparison and incorporate details of the issue record along with the books actually available on the shelves so that a comprehensive picture of the available books emerges. All books being issued or returned have to be shelved as soon as possible and rectification of stocks is to be made a regular service in order to maintain the efficiency of the computerised system.

Parallel run is a process of testing the reliability of a computerised system while retaining the manual system side by side. It reduces the risk factor since in case of any failure the existing system may be relied upon. As far as university libraries are concerned, the arrangement of books on the shelves as well as catalogue cards remains the same in both the manual and computerised systems. Computer only accelerates the speed of search and offers delivery of information in varied sequences.

In case the system works trouble free, the manual system is withdrawn and the library becomes fully automated. The degree of automation depends upon the automation of functions. Once a database is created and utilised successfully, the next step may be to barcode the library collection as well as user's IDs for auto charging and return. Some libraries in the West have computerised even the delivery of books from the shelves with the help of robot.

Data in a computerised form is the end product of a long exercise and it works as a source for all the operations of the libraries. Such data on the disk of the computer system is always exposed to risk of viruses and other hazards. There are many reasons for loss of the entered data and the risk factor is comparatively higher in the environment of university libraries where suitably trained computer professionals are few in number and the systems are to be operated by many persons.

There are many methods of data security and the most common of them is its copying from time to time on floppies or CDs. Viruses generally come through floppies and CDs brought from outside or from the Internet connection, therefore the use of such alien items be avoided as far as possible. It should also be made a regular exercise to run anti-virus software on the systems to free disk from the viruses. Entry of unauthorized users can be restricted by incorporating provision of passwords for the hardware as well as software.

Database creation should be the first and the foremost responsibility of university libraries since it allows optimum use of the resources available in an individual library and makes resource sharing possible on national as well as international level. There are some problems which may be solved by careful analysis of the work and a step by step approach for creation of the database.

Circulation division of a University library covers a variety of tasks. It works like a public relations department in a big organization. The impression about the efficiency of library service is formed here in the minds of the users. Basically, it is a technical function requiring high managerial skill. Circulation deals with the membership procedure, provides latest status of the issue able documents and keep suitable checks for safety of the collection wherever necessary. It also takes care of the routine matters of a library such as record management, display of recent additions, recalling the outstanding books, inter library lending, preparation of statistics of issue and return etc.

There are many method of circulation. The simplest among them is the ledger system. But it is no longer suitable for big libraries. In this system, details about issuing documents are copied on to the issue register each time the documents are issued. Similarly, the record is updated while retrieving them. It makes the system cumbersome and time taking. The ledger has some advantages too. Remainders can be generated easily to the borrowers for return of documents as and when required since the issue record of a borrower is available at a particular place like the bank account in ledger.

Nowadays, most of the University libraries use borrowers cards in place of ledger. It takes less time in charging and discharging of documents. In the larger libraries where daily transaction exceeds one hundred volume the introduction of card system becomes unavoidable. It is best suited to the specific needs of the University libraries. Borrowers are provided cards in accordance with the number of books allowed to be issued out. The card system increases the speed of issue and return of documents since nothing is required to be noted down in the process of charging and discharging.

The card system is based on merging details regarding the borrowers with that of books or the other issue able documents. The borrower cards contain name, status, address and instructions to the users whereas the book cards enlist particulars of books such as accession number, call number, author, title etc.

The automation of the circulation function of a University library is one of the most difficult tasks. This is all because of the complications involved in the procedure. Unlike bigger public and private libraries, there are many specific problems of the University libraries. They have many categories of users as well as the issue able documents. The users are categorized according to their status. The pre-university and undergraduates students are allowed the minimum number of books whereas the research scholars are generally eligible for the maximum. Similarly, teachers are divided according to their designations.

In the University libraries, materials are generally shelved in more than one sequences viz textbooks, reference collections, rare, reserved and non-book materials. All of them may not be issue able. The members may also not have free access to them. Further, the membership record of the University libraries changes every year as a sizeable number of students leave the institution. The newly admitted are provided fresh membership. This necessiates the updation of the membership file at frequent intervals. There always exists a possibility of pilferage of the educational materials through unauthorized means. As a precautionary measure, this is restricted by introducing codes and colour schemes and also by renewing the borrowers cards periodically.

The University libraries also face a very common problem of loss of the borrowers tickets by their members. The bigger libraries where membership runs into thousands have no effective solution to it. Once a card goes in the hand of a borrower, the library has no mechanism to cancel it or stop issuing books against it before the end of the session. The expected amount of monetary loss can also not be fixed for realization from the members. On the other hand, there are occasions when a member whose card has been misplaced demands a No Dues certificate from the library being agreed to deposit the cost of the book issued against such card. In the existing manual system of charging there is no provision to retrieve such books or fix their cost for recovery. The effective answer to this problem lies in an automated circulation of documents. .Suitable provisions have to be incorporated in software packages to deal with such problems.

On the pattern of card system, two database files are created for automated circulation of books. They contain details of members and documents respectively. In an already computerized library, the details about books are imported from the existing database and manipulated as per the needs. The membership information is collected and maintained in the circulation division in the form of a separate database which is created and updated locally. The greatest hurdles in automation of the circulation function is the non-availability of the documents file in the computerized form in most of the University libraries. This is not an easy job since it comprises of the full accession information and requires data entry of all the existing record about the issue able documents. This file goes on increasing with the addition of new documents as details about each of them are entered in it.

For the first time in cur country, the British Council Division Library in New Delhi has achieved complete automation. They use barcodes for tracking, issue and return of documents and for other library functions. The system is so effective that only one staff member is able to circulate about 800 documents a day. The documents are issued and returned with a push of button which results in a flash of light. He or she may not even touch a document while charging or discharging it.

Barcodes are series of black and white bars arranged in a predefined form to represent known coded information. These codes are read by a machine and processed by a computer without the risk of human error But instant and accurate information is essential to improve activities and obtain reliable results. Barcodes also provide the facilities of input of data at a faster speed even by an unskilled staff and also reliability and economy in collection of data. The British Council Library uses an indigenous software, package LIBSYS for generation of barcode labels. Two type of labels are generated one each for documents and members. The Library holds about 40,000 books with an annual intake of nearly 5000. They also weed out the equal number of documents every year. The first and the foremost condition for automation of the circulation function is that the information should be available in the electronic form both for the documents as well as members.

At this juncture, a semi-automated system of circulation is an effective answer. The University libraries already maintain records of the borrowers on membership cards and file them systematically. Complete information about a particular borrower is retrieved immediately if there is a demand for the same. The fully automated libraries also maintain such record on paper in addition to their active database and usually revert to them in the event of failure of the computerized system. The key to such record is the membership number allotted to the borrower in an ascending order. From the document side, the accession number has a central position just like the membership number in case of the borrowers.

In case it is not affordable for a University library to mount all its accession record on computer and to generate barcodes for them an alternate approach can be adopted for automation of the circulation function. The available accession record can be transferred on to computer copying it page by page. It can also be reproduced in micro form through the photographic process. It is worth mentioning here that the accession information is needed rarely in full by the circulation department and in this way it can be presented as and when required.

The University libraries have to clear a huge backlog of work as a pre-requisite to automation. Many services suffer because of it. The first and the foremost requirement of automation is the conversion of retrospective and current bibliographic data in the electronic form. It provides a base for computerization. The function of circulation can be automated at various levels depending upon the necessities of a library and the availability of suitable infrastructure. Many special problems pertaining to the circulation of documents in the University libraries can be solved by application of computer, fully or partially

PRESERVATION OF MANUSCRIPTS

According to Harold's Glossary, 'Manuscript' is a document of any kind which is written by hand, or text of a music or literary composition in handwritten or typescript form, and which in that form has not been reproduced in multiple copies'. Manuscripts are the original sources of human history available on various kinds of media like stones, clay tablets, palm leaves, metal leaves, tree bark, animal skin, cloth, paper etc. They have been preserved by the gone by generations for their posterity to present a true picture of the past.

The contents of manuscripts available in the advanced countries have already been explored and exploited well for the benefit of mankind but it is not so in case of the oriental manuscripts, which are far greater in number than their occidental counterparts. They also represent a more ancient and far advanced civilization that transformed records of knowledge in proportionately larger number of documents. In India, huge collections of manuscripts available in Sanskrit, Pali, Prakrat, Persian, Arabic, Urdu and Hindi languages need proper introduction to the outside world although a large number of them has already been taken out of the country by the foreign invaders.

Presently there are about 50 major collections of manuscripts available in the Indian libraries which are mainly housed at Saraswati Mahal Library, Tanjavur, Adyar Library, Madras, Khuda Bakhsh Oriental Public Library, Patna, Raza Library, Rampur, Maulana Azad Library of the Aligarh Muslim University, Asiatic Society, Kolkata, National Museum Karanchi, Salarjung Museum, Hyderabad and at many other places like Chennai, New Delhi, Bhopal, Lahore, (Now in Pakistan) Gaya, Tonk etc. In addition, many other institutions are also actively engaged in collection and preservation of manuscripts. Indira Gandhi National Centre for the Arts (IGNCA), New Delhi, Indian Institute of Advanced Studies, Simla and Library of Tibetan Works and Archives (LTWA), Dharamshala hold large collections of cultural resources in the form of manuscripts in various Indian languages. There are about 70,000 manuscripts available with LTWA only. Similarly, IGNCA is developing a collection of over one Lakh objects and illustrated miniatures in Indian and foreign collections. These include manuscripts from Victoria and Albert Museum, Chester Betty Collection. Indian National Trust for Cultural Heritage (INTACH) etc.

The worst injury an invader thought he could inflict on a country was to burn down it's libraries. When the treasury is to the economy of the nation the library is to its culture; indeed the library represents its cultural treasury. Since there was no printing press then, there would not be many copies available of works, and of some works there would be only a single copy. To destroy the library of the nation, containing rare works, would be a greater outrage than looting its treasury or dishonoring its women.

The great political upheavals in the history deprived the society of the past pride in the form of manuscripts but they proved to be life giving events also. The owners on the manuscripts remained aware of the their value through out the ages and carried these testimonies of human history where ever they moved. Manuscripts were mostly in possession of the royal families who were the main target of foreign invaders who tried to protect them in the adverse circumstances. The political instability in the Far East forced the families of its rulers to settle in India because of its prosperity in the medieval ages. Similarly, when Delhi Kingdom weakened, the families of past rulers moved to Lucknow, Hyderabad, Rampur, Bhopal, Lahore etc. in search of a better future. They moved along with their ancestral properties including manuscripts since they were regarded as symbols of royalty and a great source of respite in the adverse conditions.

It is believed that Westerners took with them some of our science manuscripts pertaining to the art of warfare. It is further claimed that Hitler made some type of weapons and aircraft on the basis of knowledge contained in these texts. The Englishmen and Frenchmen had a thirst for knowledge and research and were anxious to learn even from foreign sources. The Germans came to India and searched for palm-leaf manuscripts to take home with them. We must be grateful to some of these foreigners through whose efforts a number of our sastras were rediscovered. There was, for example, Mackenzie who was surveyor-general of the country. He went from place to place to collect palm-leaf manuscripts. There was at that time no special department to deal with them but Mackenzie had them read by experts and took steps to have them preserved, Mackenzie's men even went to Matha at Kumbakonam to gather information.

There are palm-leaf manuscripts still with us like Bhojaraja's Samarangana Sutra. From these we leam that we had long ago not only 'astras' to be employed with mantras but also "sastras" that were product of science. Digests like Varahamihira's Brhatsamhita bring together the various disciplines of our land. Some of our ancient palm-leaf manuscripts contain texts not only of our religious systems but also of various arts and sciences. Also the Puranas But we have lost many of our Sthala Puranas. We must do our best to preserve what remains and, at the same time, continue the search for more manuscripts. Moving to the medieval history period of the history one finds that a larger number of manuscripts are available in public and private collections, which need to be introduced to the masses since it may through new light on the historical past. For this purpose, there is a need of preservation.

In the old days palm-leaf manuscripts were preserved in almost-every house. They contained the texts of the epics, the Puranas, Sthala Puranas, and so on. When the palm-leaves were in danger of being damaged, their contents would be copied with a stylus on new leaves. The damaged leaves would be consigned to sacred rivers, or to some pond on the occasion of festivals.

Our forefathers went on inscribing on palm-leaves with their stylus until their hands ached. They copied old texts to be preserved for posterity. This tradition lasted until perhaps the time of our fathers. People of our generation have thrown these precious manuscripts into the river without making copies of them. So much so it is doubtful whether the texts of many Puranas will ever be available to us. Not only Puranas, but also a number of sastras. However, some scholars have taken great pains to go from place to place to collect manuscripts and preserve them in libraries. The Sarasvati Mahal Library in Tanjavur, the Oriental Manuscripts Library and the Adyar Library, Chennai, have good collections of manuscripts. The Theosophical Society Library, Adyar, has done commendable work in this respect. Sarabhoji and other rulers of Tanjavur took great interest in their preservation. During the Mughal period, manuscripts were regularly copied under the royal patronage in order to preserve their contents for the future generations.

With the passage of time, new type of materials emerged which were used as medium for manuscripts such as metal sheets, animal skin, paper etc. but they all have a definite life span and more physical limitations. The digital media has taken advantage on all the previous media for preservation of manuscripts. It is not only more durable but offers a number of added advantages.

The technological advancements have led to better ways for preservation of manuscripts without loosing their originality. There is an added advantage of the modern methods of preservation over the traditional ones. By the new methods, the manuscripts in their original form may not be needed for consultation and its images may be made available to the users. Thus not only the life of the manuscript will be prolonged but also it would be easier to offer it to the researchers or the public as the case may be. Internet has emerged the best medium for this purpose and through the provision of web, manuscripts may be made available to the outside world without compromising on their safety.

Previous designs of the Web were focused on providing general information because of the limitation of speed and memory of computer systems but the trend has drastically changed. Now memory is not a problem and even video coverage, which occupies a lot of computer space can be accommodated in larger quantity. Manuscripts being still pictures do not need much space as compared to video and systems with extended hard disc memory can be used for an average collection of manuscripts for storage and display of information resources on the Net.

Document imaging is the most appropriate method for converting manuscripts into digital form. Digital cameras are used for this purpose. It facilitates speed in the work and shows them in their original form as a manuscript looks like. Earlier, expert calligraphers were employed to copy them but it was a very time taking and costly affair. Moreover, there are scripts which arc no more in use and neither computer will accept them if keyed in nor they can easily be copied by calligraphers while converting manuscripts, miniature etc. in digital form, reference can be maintained side by side just as the inventory of photographs is developed. Systems with extended memory can be used for storage and retrieval of the vast quantity of information. Libraries in the past were worried about the adverse climatic conditions, which destroy them. This fear has also been eliminated as the digital recording may last for centuries in the adverse weather conditions.

Using the web as medium for research in case of manuscripts is much more advantageous for preservation as well as research. Earlier they could be consulted by only those researchers who had means to travel long distance where the manuscripts were located. The timings of consultation were also limited. But on the web, now such manuscripts can be referred to as and when needed by any one and from any corner of the world. Moreover, they can be made available to countless of users simultaneously and can be archived and stay on line for indefinite period. The web is an effective means of two-way communication. It makes the process of give and take easier. Ones own resources or queries may be floated on the net in order to know the reactions from all over the world. Many a researchers make appeal for collecting the relevant information on their topics of study. The same approach may be adopted in case of manuscripts.

About all major libraries of the world holding the oriental manuscripts such as India Office Library, Chester Betty Library, Cambridge University Library etc. can be hooked up on the Internet. Web provides innumerable references to the oriental collections that present a wide choice of selection to the researchers. Recently, some research engines were used to surf the resources available on the web. The term 'oriental manuscripts' was a search string. It delivered about 30,599 references through google.com whereas hotbot.com located about 37,500 such items. Moreover, these resources are not the ultimate as they contain sub fields and also refer to many related links dealing with the similar contents. The Web works like a reference librarian automatically. If some one is not satisfied with the presentation of one search engine then it provides option to try the others and it is very likely that the relevant information is located from one or the other source.

Most of the oriental libraries of the Indian subcontinent employ manual methods of retrieval of information from manuscripts in their possession. They generally maintain details on ledgers, hand list, catalogue cards etc. and need the services of subject specialists in most of the cases because of the limitations no single person can achieve mastery in respect of the larger collections of libraries holding manuscripts.

There is an urgent need for mounting all the resources and reference tools regarding manuscripts on computer such as hand list, ledger and catalogues and descriptions in whatever form they are available so that they may be made available for the outside world through the Web.

The web medium can also be used to provide the researchers, educators and library professionals access to resources which they otherwise might not have known existed. Materials stored in close collections can be displayed digitally if not allowed to be accessed in their original form. However, restrictions may also be imposed to the extent possible in view of safety and security of the manuscripts and also for commercialisation if intended. There are provisions for displaying only the reference or the text or both of them as the case may be. The transfer of manuscripts from one place to another has also become economic, easier and faster with the help of new information technology.

Manuscripts are the invaluable sources of the history and cultural heritage. They need to be preserved properly while keeping in view their utility. The climatic conditions and delay in application of information technology pose a serious threat to the existence of manuscripts for which the new electronic media can be an effective solution.

12

Internet, Intranet and Homepaging

In higher education a library caters to the academic and research needs of the students and faculty and facilitates independent learning. It works like a backbone for generation of new knowledge. A distinguished Vice Chancellor of a modem University of England, Sir Charles Grant Robertson, once said, "If 1 wore a dictator, I would reduce the time devoted to lectures to a third of that usually occupied by them and insist on the students spending three hours every day in the library". Similarly, various commissions set up on higher education in India have attributed great value to the university libraries. Kothari Commission in its report has emphasized the importance of libraries in higher education. It asserts "No university, college or department should be set up without taking into account its library needs in terms of staff, books, journals, space etc. Nothing could be more damaging to a growing department than to neglect its library or to give it a low priority. On the contrary, the library should be an important centre of attraction of the college or university campus". The National Policy on Education has further emphasized the need for a better library service in the time to come.

Internet can play a significant role in higher education. The downslide in the economic graph of the country has added to the problems of the university libraries. On the one side is the ever-increasing literary warrant on all subjects of study while on the other hand, the purchasing power of our currency is eroding in the national as well as in the international market. The advanced countries encash the cost of their experimentation from the developing countries by way of charging higher costs of their publications that may be available in the form of books or journals or the new electronic media that are a must for undertaking new researches.

The University Grants Commission is more a funding agency rather an authority for effective control of the educational institutions. This also adds to the problems of the libraries since universities easily divert funds allocated for the libraries for other purposes. The special grants for automation of the university libraries was released to all the universities but their impact remains almost unseen. Generations after generations of computer emerged and met extinction but most of the libraries could not be computerized. At the university teaching level also, this phenomenon is evident. Despite clear recommendations for adoption of the Curriculum Development Committee report, only a few institutions have implemented the same.

University libraries have been great losers in the era of information explosion. In the vent of economic crises in the universities, libraries are looked upon as scapegoats. Librarians also have not yet popularized the library services and made the academic community aware of the important role. They can play in the changing environment. Even today they insist on continuation of the traditional systems for delivery of information whereas the libraries are the most dynamic institutions like the disciplines of technology and medicine. They can play the role of a catalyst for promotion of research, since the knowledge first knocks at their doors and is later diverted to the area of the actual need. So far, they have remained confined to books and the other forms of printed materials. Many technologies emerged and vanished in the mean-while just as the audiovisual media flourished within the last fifty years but no visible impact could be seen on the university libraries. Similar is the case of computer application.

With lack of the required technological infrastructure our university libraries are not able to deliver goods with their vast resources whereas, the conventional resources are not the only condition for a good service. The libraries of western countries have been so useful and famous that even to satisfy our indigenous needs, we, generally, consult their collections. The British Council Division Library in New Delhi with its meagre resources of 40,000 books and the latest information technology at their disposal, attracts over 1,000 readers a day and it transacts about 750 books daily. They are having a professional staff of eight only and the in-house functions besides processing of the new arrivals, issue and return, they discard and add about 5,000 books annually. The proper and economic use of the information resources can also be seen in the libraries attached to the private entrepreneurs. In this regard, the library owned by Living Media India, New Delhi can be cited as an example. Our libraries with more manpower and vast resource have failed to achieve such excellence. It is true that our university libraries have failed in application of technologies at a proper time that could have made them more prominent organs within the institutions.

For judicious application of information technology in the university libraries, there is a compelling need of creating systems cadre that may be drawn from the hard-core of the profession like the sections dealing with the technical processing of documents/ their acquisition and stock verification and also the existing facilities provided in the name of computerization. Of late, there is an awareness among the librarians to modernize the university libraries and they have established automation committees but computerizing alone is not going to deliver the goods at this stage. The agony of the university libraries is that they are neither the department of teaching nor disassociated with the academic work. Unlike the teaching department/ where decisions about the functioning and development of the departments are jointly taken on a common platform shared by all the faculty members, a library is more under one head who alone may or may not be competent enough to meet the challenges of the time. It leaves lesser scope for the others to contribute to it meaningfully. India has established its lead in software development on the international level all because of its younger generation. Then there seems to be no reason for a failure if the same yardstick is applied to the library field also by giving proper opportunity to the libraries. Though we have enough resources, they are not shared judiciously for innovation and development.

INTERNET

The latest advances in computers, telecommunications and Internet have made circumstances more conducive for the universities to adopt new information technologies in the teaching and learning process of students thus making the method of instruction more interactive and effective. But in spite of the facilities available, cost effectiveness of the new educational media and its suitability to the perception process of man, the potentiality of the electronic media is not being utilized for education properly. The libraries in advanced countries are accommodating all types of media and providing services to their clientele. John S. Teague, Librarian Emeritus, City University Library, London realized this necessity about 15 years back when he wrote, "print on paper must be regarded as just one of the physical media which carry information. Other media are microfilm, magnetic tape, magnetic disc, videotape, videodisc, electromagnetic tape, pulses of light in fibre optic cables etc." (Microfilm video and electronic media-librarianship. London, Butterworths, 1985). But, most of the Indian universities barring a few in the south have remained almost unaffected by this change.

The present philosophy of library service that requires the users to come to the library will no longer dominate. In the time to come, the mode of delivery of information will change with increasing number of universities offering courses of study online. Librarians will also meet the particular needs of off-campus students. This could have been a dream about a decade ago but it is a reality now.

Computerization remained the first preference of the universities in their policies during the decades of 80's and 90's when it finally succumbed to the superiority of Internet. A computer is effective only in reflecting and utilizing one's in-house resources whereas Internet with its worldwide connection is more powerful and economic for the educational institutions.

The rapid development of digital network all over the globe during the last 20 years has promoted communication of information at a mind-boggling speed. This has proved comparatively more fruitful for library and information centres compared with any other organization, for it offers economy in storage, search and utility of information. Internet was invented about thirty years ago. In the early days it was mainly used by scientists, working in the common areas of research. It was not so user-friendly as we see it today. Now, the browsers require only a few clicks on easily figured icons and links to ride a whole ocean of information.

Internet became more popular by its feature of the World Wide Web in 1991, Tim Berners-Lee, a young scientist working in European Particle Physics Laboratory (CERN) produced Internet's first browser. According to him, "the dream behind the Web is of a common information space in which we communicate by sharing information. "By its application, someone could scan every document or photo or video on the net. It gave an opportunity to share the resources by individuals and organizations on the basis of mutual understanding. In the past ten years, it has been so popular that the number of Internet users has jumped from 600,000 to 140 million and it is expected to grow further to 350 millions within the next three years.

Now, Internet has emerged as the most powerful medium for storage and retrieval of information. It works round the clock and connects every nook and corner of the globe. With an unprecedented growth in the quantum of knowledge worldwide and the easy accessibility, Internet has become an unavoidable necessity for every institution of higher learning and research.

So great is the impact of Internet that even the textbook industry is going to witness a fundamental shift leave alone the periodical publications and the other forms of print media. Once a sizeable number of traders agree for sharing ideas electronically along with a higher percentage of students having access to personal computers, the situation will be quite different. Having textbooks available electronically at lower cost will enable cash strapped institutions to redirect money spent on printed textbooks for other needs. The faster the growth of technology the shorter is the time to apply it for proper gains.

The present situation has become an ideal one for adoption of Internet as in the words of Bill Gates "For the first time, all kinds of information-numbers, text sound video-can be put into a digital form that any computer can now store, process and forward. For the first time, standard hardware combined with a standard software platform has created economies of scale that make powerful computing solutions available extensively to all kinds of companies" (Business @ the speed of thought: Penguin Books: London :1999).

The expenses being incurred on the university libraries can conveniently be reduced to half in case the potential of Internet is utilized properly. It is a good substitute to a huge number of reference tools, journals and books. Moreover, the updated information is instantly available on it all the time. Like in the area of medicine, efforts on international level are on to serve humanity in the field of education. New web sites are being launched on Internet day by day for education of the masses. They may be visited on will with out any barrier and the information contained in them can be downloaded for future use.

Internet connectivity is easily available and affordable for most of the universities and colleges as the cost of computer hardware, software and connectivity has come down considerably during the last few years. Moreover, there has been standardization in the ever-changing configuration of systems. The software has been made more user friendly for computer as well as netsurfing. Now, the services are also being offered through cable TV and in case this facility widens there will be no need to purchase the computer hardware and software at all.

In most of the university libraries. Internet is more a showpiece and status symbol rather than a useful tool for search of the vital information. Looking at the central universities located in the northern part of the country one can easily notice that the facility exists in most of the libraries but it is not being utilized properly.

Libraries can make use of the huge literary and media resources available on Internet. Most of them are offered free of cost and in case of the priced items, the cost is comparatively lower than their printed counterparts. One such resource is Encarta Encyclopaedia published by M/S Microsoft Inc., which costs L 39.99 only.

The Encarta 99 Encyclopaedia Deluxe Edition contains the following information that may require an average library collection to provide:

(a) About 5,000 new or updated, articles

(b) Media including images, sounds, videos, and interactive charts

(c) Links to more than 8,500 informative sites on the World Wide Web

(d) Article updates and Web Links that can be downloaded using a modem

(e) virtual tours with panoramic views of places to explore

(f) New Interactivities

(g) Interactive Collages

(h) Research organizer to help to collect and organize information for reports of the research projects

(i) Encarta Resource Centre, providing ideas and advice on using the encyclopaedia as a learning resource

(j) The Timeline of world history, showing historical development with the time

(k) Atlas

(l) The Mind Maze game that is an educational quiz programme available on various subjects of study

(m) Topic trails

(n) Side bars, including guest essays

(o) Call-Out Quotes

(p) Further Reading

(q) Closed captions

Following are the broad categories of resources that can be accessed on Internet –

* Internet Yellow Pages
* Online Dictionaries
* Digital Encyclopaedias
* Manuals and Handbooks
* Digital maps
* Online Travel Guides
* Patents
* Almanacs
* Standards
* Quotes Collection
* Online Glossaries
* Biographical Sources

In the university libraries, the highest portion of library budget, apart from salaries of staff is spent on subscription of journals. The back issues are generally purchased paying higher cost. But there is hardly any library, which conducts utility and productivity surveys so that the fact about the usefulness of the resources as well as the services may come out and be known to the academic community. Internet is an effective substitute to a large collection of books and journals. Periodical publications in almost all the disciplines of study are available online. The original thoughts in them do not take much time to be publicized and updated as in the case of the print media. Only one channel is involved here in the production of the documents and that is of the author who can reach readers worldwide within no time. Collective and organized efforts are also being made to bring such publications in the electronic media just as in case of the publications on paper. Information is available in plenty and it is only the matter of selection that is more important and rewarding. In the time to come, one may expect still better consolidation of resources because of the enhancement of computer memory, speed and increasing coordination among the service providers. .

Internet can be used in the university libraries right from the selection of documents to delivery of information to the end user. Various search engines, flash news of the bibliographic items ranging from books to cassettes, CD ROMs and the educational software available online. One such a store is amazon.com that is also called 'the paradise of books'. It gives information in detail about these items and their marketing. It also works like a 'prenetal catalogue' for librarians that makes them aware about the forthcoming publications.

It is not advisable to insist for particular journals that are available online but a serious study of the contents of the maximum possible number of journals should be made to select the most appropriate ones or their substitutes. It is quite possible that there are many titles available on the same subject. The sample copies of the priced journals are also available to scan.

Searching information on Internet is like having a talk with some friend since it is highly interactive and user friendly. Once, somebody establishes connection, the interface encourages for more and more information. This process becomes never ending and ever satisfying for the users. One's own limitations of time or resources may be the barrier for the work ahead, and not the paucity of information. With the ever-emerging user-friendly software,

Internet has become a child's play, so much involving and attractive that it remains ever half-played.

The basic principles of library science are applied in almost all the functions of organization and retrieval of the contents. The most relevant segments of the desired information is retrieved as the first in sequence. Similarly, in most of the cases of search, the subject or key words on the required subjects are given to Internet as "Search String".

The collection of user's profiles and their maintenance for pinpointed service is an important task. Every user is not expected to be an expert of Internet. Moreover, there may be conditions that do not allow free access to all. In that case, user's profiles can give an idea to collect materials on the relevant topics through a questionnaire. In their profiles, they should be asked to write a few key words and also the summary of their research projects. Then the Selective Dissemination of Information (SDI) may be initiated. When this effort gets success, which is bound to do so the next step should be to target the final year postgraduate and undergraduate students respectively who are assigned projects. Similarly, the facility may be generalized by providing the required number of terminals for the remaining students also.

The libraries should also maintain a list of the related web sites. It can easily be achieved by inviting the user's attention and an appeal to share the experiences of users with the library staff so that the benefit of the individual efforts is popularized among the general users. This will save the time of users since they may go to the web sites directly instead of coining search strings and making stray efforts. In university libraries, Internet can be used for the following purposes:

- Browsing brochures of academic and research organizations
- Consulting library catalogues
- Buying and browsing electronic journals, research reports, books, videos CDs etc.

- Reading newspapers
- Deciding topics of research work and obtaining feedback
- Taking part in discussions and
- Building corporate image among the similar organizations.

The newest media available over Internet is the World Wide Web popularly known s WWW or W3. It is a huge collection of interconnected hypertext documents, which contain links to oilier documents, files and sites on the Internet. With a web browser, all these resources are accessible. There are a number of pages on the Web that offer one of the two models for finding specific information. One model is that of a directory, where web sites are organized by topics and sub topics just as in the schemes of library classification. One has to start from a subject in general and then proceed to specific concepts. There are a number of directories available on Internet. The most common among them are as below :

* Yahoo: http://www.yahoo.com
* Alta Vista : http://www.altavista.com
* Hotbot: http://www.hotbot.corn
* Easy Search: http:/ /www.easysearch.com
* Lycos: http://www.lycos.com
* One Look ; http://www.onelook.com
* Web Crawler : http://www.webcrawler.com
* Excite: http://www.excite.com
* Infoseek: http://www.infoseek.com

The other method of search is through the searchable index, where a key word is entered on the desired subject and the search page gives a list of suggested sites that can be accessed further. It is a good substitute to a huge mass of the subject catalogue of libraries. The method of approach is almost similar for both, but Internet is far superior for it needs no standard subject headings to be formulated first and then to retrieve the document. Internet with its vast memory and speed retrieves the desired information in a fraction of time. Further, the search can be narrowed down by selecting the specific areas and asking the system to do.

To look for a specific university library on Internet, the library catalogues arranged geographically may be consulted first and then shifted to geographical regions. The next step may be start zooming for the particular library someone is looking for. This will follow the login instruction to connect and interact with the specific library located anywhere in the world. A programme called hytelnet has a fairly up-to-date list of university libraries. The hytelnet is accessible at http://library.usask.ca/hytelenet/.

The Internet Public Library at http://www.ipl.org, apart from making available resources to the users provides guidelines for the general public as well as the professional librarians and information specialists in collection building and the use of its resources. Some other agencies also help in collection building and retrieval functions.

An additional advantage in education and research is that Internet is also a very economic and a fast means for establishing contact with the people. Taking advantage of this facility, experts in various disciplines of study have come together. They cannot only communicate with each other through e-mail but can also discuss the problems together by chatting and video conferencing.

In the changed environment of today, the libraries have to give due weightage to access information rather than holding larger collections. University libraries should try to explore the Internet resources. For this, every library should achieve Internet connectivity and make the students and teachers aware of the important resources and services available. They may maintain user profiles and the directory of websites related to their specific needs. The library staff may also be trained in the skill of information search although it is not required necessarily since they are already trained in organization and processing and retrieval of information and only some basic will suffice their needs.

INTRANET

An Intranet is a private system that uses computer hardware and software specially developed to provide communication, information management and information publishing services within an organization. An organization, which has many computers usually owns and operates a private network that connects all the computers. Such a network is called Intranet. It is independent of any external support but to provide Internet services, an Intranet is connected with Internet Unlike public access networks, Intranet is restricted to provide security. Only authorized computers at the organization can be connected to it. The restrictions allow computers inside the organization to exchange information but keep the information confidential and protected from outsiders.

Libraries attached to education and research organizations are in the fore front of using computers for collecting, storing and dissemination of information. Most of the university libraries have mounted references and resources on computers and are also offering services in a networked environment being larger in respect of size of collection, decentralization and interdisciplinary nature of researches being undertaken within them.

As Intranet is a connecting device for many computers within an organization it can solve many problems related to input, storage and dissemination of information without much inconvenience. The other services expected from Intranet are the following

1. World Wide Web publishing
2. File Transfer Protocol
3. Indexing and Searching Services
4. Facility to run scripts

Intranet if employed in a larger set up like the Library of a major organization will bring efficiency in work and help improve the standard of education and research. The following are the advantages for the university libraries :

* It will connect all libraries/departments of the University
* It will be a private network
* It will provide connectivity round the clock
* It will permit decentralization of the library work, like accessioning, classification, cataloguing etc.
* It will allow resources sharing within the campus including the stored data and e-journals
* It is cost effective since only one software package can be used for the entire library system.
* It will provide connectivity from and to the libraries to residence of the authorized users
* Recording and dissemination of information/meetings/lectures from any location
* Data is secured from external risks

Besides the above advantages, the facility may be used for other purposes like vigilance and security of the campus.

The basic requirements for installation of an Intranet are computer hardware, software and a connecting device.

Intranet is based on a client server system where the server is a computer that has the following functions:

* Running the Intranet service software
* Storing some or all of the content that is available to the users

The requirements of the server computer depend upon the number of connections expected to be provided per hour. For a few hundred connections, a Pentium 4 with 1.6 Gh speed, 64 MB RAM and 40 GB memory is more than sufficient. In case the load increases on the sever, users will find them waiting for retrieval of information. The capacity of a computer system may be enhanced by adding more memory and processors and splitting the contents among them.

Software for the Intranet is available in two categories, the server software and the client software.

Intranet needs a server software that runs a computer and provides services such as World Wide Web publishing and File Transfer besides indexing and searching facilities. Server software is available on the Internet free of cost and the commercial packages such as Microsoft's Internet Information Server and Netscape Navigator are available for a variety of operating systems including UNIX and Windows NT server.

The software that runs a client is called a browser, which is used to access and browse Web pages. It may also be acquired free of cost or at a reasonably low cost. The most popular server is Netscape Navigator Some other browsers are also available at the Web addresses in Table 1.

Intranet is a gold mine of free software One can find any type of software to run a full featured Intranet service but the software downloaded from Internet should be used with great care. It is always better to take precautions and invest some money for a well designed, listed and supported software.

Table 1. Web Address of Browsers

S. No.	*Name*	*Web Address*
1.	Midas WWW	http:/www.midas.slac.stanford.edu/ midas22/introduction.html
2.	Mosaic	ftp://ftp.ncsa.uiuc.edu/mosaic
3.	Netscape	htt://home.netscape.com
4.	Emacs	ftp://mouse.cs.indiana.edu/pub/elips/w3
5.	Lynx	ftp://ftp2.cc.ukans.edu/pub/lynx/
6.	Internet Explorer	http://www.microsoft.com

A connecting device provides links between the server and the client. It is mainly based on the following two devices

* Networking Device capable of running on radio frequencies
* RF Links comprising of Mast and Antennas

There are many devices, which can be used to connect a server with browser but their usage depends upon the convenience and the financial resources of an organization to install and support the device The geographical location of the various departments of an organization is to be taken into consideration because sometimes it is hard to manage the connections besides being in the position of installation of the costlier systems.

The most significant feature of this proposal is that it does not require a major expenditure and utilizes the existing hardware of the library systems. Most of the software are available on Internet free of cost. The expenditure is to be incurred mainly on the connecting device.

Wireless SS Device may be used for connecting servers with browsers in a situation when physical connectivity is hard to achieve and maintain. The device is based on router plus antenna that generate and receive signals, which activate the computers installed at both the ends. Once installed the device is almost maintenance free. The cost of the device is based on the number of locations. For one location it costs Rs. 1.5 lacs plus the expenditure to be made on erection of an antenna tower at the low visibility points for which the additional expenditure is Rs. 1,850 per meter.

It is better to take up the project in a phased manner connecting more significant points at first and then extending the facility to the less used libraries. This will reduce the expenses at one time. Additional facilities like audio and video conferencing and installation of video cameras for security checks etc. may be introduced at a later stage.

Intranet like Internet is a very significant system of information. It is being used for many purposes but hardly installed for the university libraries which are the largest body of information within an academic and research institution. There is no much cost involved for two or three points of communication as the usual additional expenditure for one location is about 1.5 lacs, which an average university library can afford. The existing hardware of computer can be utilized with the software available form the Internet free of cost.

HOME PAGING

Information has played a key role in the development of society. The experiences of mankind came down to the posterity through the communication of ideas by different means. *As* the human society progressed, the barriers of time and space in spread of information were removed

Internet has brought a significant change in the environment of learning. It offers a vast array of information resources. People turn to Internet for news, mails, business and educational facilities. It is being user-friendly day by day and the access has now been extended from computers to laptops and mobile phones also.

Internet is continuously growing internationally. Within the last one decade, its services have spread among of the word. In 1991, it was within the reach of 73 countries only but by 1995 it reached 148 countries. The number of Internet users is also growing tremendously. It almost doubles after every two years. The scope of Internet is also widening as it is being used for publishing of ideas apart from being an effective tool for storage aid retrieval of information.

The concept of homepage along with the World Web, also known as the Web, WWW or W3. The term has multiple meanings. The sense in which it is used today is not the same as used in the past. Earlier, being represented by many terms, a homepage now refers to the first page of a website or the page which is approached first by a searcher while connected with a website. It is also the page, which is referred to in the website repeatedly as the search within the website generally starts afresh from the homepage.

In context of a university, a homepage contains the most needed information searched by students, faculty and others for the various reasons ranging from admissions to the result of examination. A homepage can be compared with the main menu of a user-friendly computer software which encourages interaction and promotes its use by presenting the contents in a logical order.

A homepage establishes the identity of an individual or organization on the net and is like putting up a flag for someone in the cyberspace. It is the Guttenberg's press of our time with extended facility for low cost publishing. Anyone cab publish any kind of information including text, graphics, sound and video or a combination of all on the web through the homepage. It opens the doors of the millions of Internet users all over the world to receive ideas floated by someone. A homepage can be a full service front and for an organization. Here we restrict to discuss a home page about the universities only.

A homepage is needed for global recognition of an individual or organization. Universities stand for teaching, research and extension and what distinguishes them from college is the facility for research. Higher the intended level of research in an academic institution, more is the need for a good information system that is effectively provided by homepage across the geographical boundaries of the institutions.

Information resources on Intenet are growing faster than the capability of indexers to trap them. The gap between the two is widening day by day. Therefore, all resources cannot be reached easily by the search engines alone. The universities should make special provisions for dissemination of information about them. The research queries are routed towards homepage for which suitable provisions are to be incorporated.

An unprecedented growth in the number of educational institutions and the necessity of making information easily available to the clientele out of the vast information resources that has also necessitated the availability of a homepage in order to present information about the courses offered, admission procedure and examination and also to provide relevant information on other aspects of an institution. Information presented in the homepage may be made public or restricted to be delivered on conditional basis depending upon the policy of the institution.

The basic requirements for creation of a homepage are computer, Internet connection, Web space, contents creation and file transfer.

Computer is the basic requirement for converting data into electronic form to facilitate upload and download of information with speed and accuracy. Most of the computer systems available in the market fulfill the requirements, however a PC 486 of Pentium series suits to the needs. Now a days, computers have become a necessity for the universities and about all of them are already having it which can be used for a variety of tasks including the homepage creation and hosting.

The Pre-requisite to Internet connectivity apart from computer is a telephone line and modern in order to transfer signals from and to the other computer systems. An Internet connection, which is the license to transfer information is generally of three types i.e. Dialup, Leased line and VSAT.

Availability of web space is the most significant requirement. Many Internet Service Providers (ISPs) offer web space for hosting homepages free of cost up to certain amount of memory. They generally do it for the sake of advertisements, which bring revenue. The advertisements are generally in the corners of the homepage an do not hinder the process of information exchange. The larger sites are hosted on prescribed rates.

Some major service providers, which make web space available for hosting are the following

S. No.	*Address of ISPs*
1	www. geocities.com
2	www.tripod.com
3	www.firely.com
4	www.anglefire.com
5	www.I freespace.com
6	www.webjump.com
7	www.prohosting.com
8	www.netcolony.com
9	www.netcolony.com
10	www.50megs.com

The selection of an ISP should be made with great care keeping in view the availability of the maximum free space with less area for advertisement and feasibility to cope with the future requirements of the organization. The speed of operations is equally important since it determine the loading and retrieval of information.

After reaching an agreement with ISP, the first step should be to identify some suitable terms to represent organization on the net. The terms so selected or coined have to be matched with those, which are already occupied by way of advance registration. The popular domains for universities are academic and educational, which are represented by 'ac' and 'edu' respectively. Some suitable terms may be coined, matching with the name of the universities concerned since if cleared by the 'checkdomain', such terms become the identity mark for the institution.

A thorough survey of the nature of clientele and the needs of the organization is necessary before undertaking the work of content development. This can be achieved by contact with the users of the site followed up with the usability testing to make sure that work goes in the right direction. The following guidelines may be followed in developing the contents:

1. Keeping in mind the type of content or information intended to be put on the web
2. Keeping in mind the goals for presentation of content
3. Organization of contents into main pages
4. Coming up with a general structure of pages and topics by storyboarding the homepage
5. Foreseeing readers reaction while searching the homepage
6. Avoiding having too many layers of information as users want to get information quickly and having too many steps will annoy them

The homepage may begin with general details about the institution, which can be followed by information on collection, services and staff. The collection may include books, journals and the other media while services may reflect the list of additions Current Awareness Service etc. A homepage should also offer links to the similar sites.

In order to make a homepage easy to search, a logical order of content be followed and the extensive use of graphics and colours be avoided since they hinder the speed of retrieval. The easiest way is to refer to the related websites before undertaking the work of creation. About all major universities of the world maintain homepages.

Once the contents of a homepage are finalized and put into a logical sequence on paper, they are keyed in and made available on a computer system. The task of content verification and designing is undertaken to ensure that it looks on the desired pattern while retrieving. The results can be checked on Netscape as well as Internet Explorer or on some other browsers. In case of the expected results, the next step is to transfer the contents to the web servers of an ISP. This is achieved by File Transfer Protocol (FTP).

In order to ascertain if the contents have been successfully transferred, one has to check it by typing the URL address in the local browser. The attempt is considered successful if it is retrieved on the desired pattern. While submitting a homepage, it is also necessary to assign the category of URL, descriptors and keywords. The search engines put page under various categories depending upon their descriptions. In case of universities, the popular terms : name of university, higher education, universities etc. may be assigned for search engines. Some of the most popular search engines are given below:

1. http://www.google.com.
2. http://www.yahoo.com
3. http:www.hotbot.com
4. http://www.altavista.com
5. http://www.indianindex.com
6. http://www.khoj.com
7. http:www.infoseek.com
8. http://www.lycos.com

In India, about all premier institutions have developed their websites. The addresses of some websites are given below.

S. N.	*Name of the University*	*Web Address*
1.	Aligarh Muslim University	www.amu.ac.in
2.	Allahabad University	www.allduniv.edu
3.	Anna University	www. annauniv.edu
4.	Assam University	www.assamuniv.nic.in
5.	Banaras Hindu University	www.bhu.ac.in
6.	Bangalore University	www.bangaloreuniversity.net.
7.	Cochin University	www.cusat.ac.in
8.	Devi Ahaliya Vishvavidyalaya	www.davy.ac.in
9.	Dr. B. R. Ambedkar Open University	www.braou ac.in

10.	Guru Gibind Singh Indraprasth University	www.ggsipu.nic.in
11.	Gulbarga University	www.gulbargauniversity .kar.nic
12.	Gujarat Agriculture University	www. gau.guj.nic.in
13.	Himachal Pradesh University	www.hpuniv.nic.in
14.	Indira Gandhi National Open University	www.ignou.ac.in
15.	Jamia Millia Islamia	www.Jmi.nic.in
16.	Osmania University	www.osmanial.ac.in
17.	Pondicherry University	www.pondiuniv.org
18.	Punjabi University	www.universitypunjabi.org
19.	Tamil Nadu University	www.tnuniv.ac.in
20.	University of Delhi	www.du.ac.in
21.	University of Hyderabad	www.uoh.ernet.in
22.	University of Kerala	www.keralauniv.edu
23.	University of Madras	www.unom.ac.in
24.	University of Mumbai	www.mum.ac.in
25.	University of Mysore	www.universityofmysore.com
26.	University of Pune	www.www.unipune.ernet.in
27.	University of Rajasthan	www.uniraj.org
28.	Visva-Bhatri Shantiniketan	www.visva-bharti.ac.in
29.	Vidyasagar University	www.vidyasagar.ac.in

In the academic world, netsurfing has become an affair of the masses now. People refer to the websites of universities to get information about their history, faculties, departments courses, admission, examination, library, research activities, news, staff etc. but the way of presentation of contents on the homepages and subsequent sub-pages varies from one institution to the other. In India, most of the central universities and a large number of educational institutions in the Southern part of the country have nicely developed their websites and they are increasingly being searched but the users have to undergo afresh experience while shifting from one site to the other in absence of uniformity in content presentation on the sites.

The necessity for standardization in presentation of contents is well realized now for the assistance of the users of websites. In the interest of the academic community some agencies like University Grants Commission, INFLIBNET. National Informatics Centre, Indian Bureau of Standards may undertake the work of suggesting standards for developing homepages for universities in consultation with computer and information science professionals working in the universities.

Bibliography

1. ACQUIRING MINDS WANT TO KNOW; The acquisition process of video and CD ROM. MC Jl. Of Academic Media Librarianship. 6.2: 1999. URL: http/wings.buffalo.edu/publications/mcjrnl/v6n2.alacquire.htm 1.
2. ACRL GUDELINES AND STANDARDS: URL: http://www.ala.org/acrl/euides/index.html.
3. ADLER (Rebecca). Media librarianship: curricular response to the digital revolution. MC Jl. Of Academic Media Librarianship, 5, 2:1997. URL.-http://wings.buffalo.edu./publications/mcjnl/v6nl/adler.html
4. ADLER (Richard) and CATER (Douglas). Television as a cultural force. 1976. Praeger Publishing, New York.
5. AGRAWAL (Binod C) and others. INSAT pre-production television research for higher education: A consolidated report for the University Grants Commission. 1986. UGC. Ahmedabad.
6. AICHILI (Jeaw). A manual of AACR2: examples of motion picture and video recording. 1981. Soldier Greek Press.
7. MERICAN LIBRARY ASSOCIATION. Video round table guidelines for interlibrary loan of audiovisual formats. 1998. URL: http://www.lib.virginia.edu.dmmc/vrt/illguide.html.
8. AMERICAN LIBRARY ASSOCIATION. Glossary of Library & Information Science. 1993. ALA, Chicago

9. AMERICAN LIBRARY ASSOCIATION. Introduction of automation. 1983. ALA, Chicago.
10. AMERICAN LIBRARY ASSOCIATION. World Encyclopaedia of Library and Information Science. 1993. ALA. Chicago.
11. AMJAD ALL Computerization of media libraries. Jl. of Information Sciences 3 ,19; 1993: 119-127.
12. AMJAD ALL Computerized information retrieval system for stock shots: the experience of a media library in Librarianship and Information Technology, 1992. Indian Library Association, New Delhi.
13. AMJAD ALI. Database creation for ETV production libraries in Database Production Management and Distribution. 1993. Tata-McGraw Hill, New Delhi. 338-345.
14. AMJAD ALI. Educational video: factors responsible for growth in India in Library Movement and Library Development. 1994., Indian Library Association. New Delhi.
15. AMJAD ALI. ETV and the Commonwealth of learning. University News. 35. 20; 1997; 9-11
16. AMJAD ALI. Information management in film and television libraries. Lib. Herald 32, 1-2; 1994.
17. AMJAD ALI. Information sources for ETV production. University News 32, 4; 5-8; 1994.
18. AMJAD ALI. Information system for educational video: the case of an indigenous database. AGLIS Journal. 1993.
19. AMJAD ALI. Internet and the university libraries. University News. 23 April 2001; 6-10.
20. AMJAD ALI. Motion pictures as source of information: problems of the Indian universities. University News 31. 22: 8-9; 1993.
21. AMJAD ALI. Networking of ETV agencies in Open and Distance Education. 1998. ICDE., New Delhi.

22. AMJAD ALI. Print versus electronic media: educating with economy. University News 9 May. 1993:12-16.

23. AMJAD ALI. Resource sharing among ETV libraries. University News 32, 44; 5-7 ; 1994.

24. AMJAD ALI. University libraries in the current perspective. University News 39. 48: 2001. 10-14.

25. AMJAD ALI. Video in higher education: The Indian scenario, paper contributed to the 13th National Seminar of the Society for Information Science and published in Information Management for Rural Development. 1994. Shipra Publications, New Delhi.

26. ANDERSON (HR). Selecting and developing media for instruction. New York, Van Nostrand Reinhold Co., 1976; 37-38, 47-48

27. ANGLO-AMERICAN CATALOGUING RULES. 1988. 2nd Ed. ALA, Chicago.

28. ANNA (JK). Library and society. 1987. Ess Ess Publications, New Delhi.

29. APLAN (Don). Television and classroom. 1986. Knowledge Industry Publication Inc.

30. ARAM (IA). Television in education. 1993. Sangam Books, New Delhi.

31. ARORA (J) and KAUR (S). Recent information technologies and impact on dissemination of information. ALSD. 39, 1: 1992; 12-18.

32. ARORA (Jagdish) and SRIVASTAVA (JP). Application of recent information technology for information management: An Indian Scenario. AGLIS Journal. 11, 1995; 1-14.

33. ARUNA (A). Online Public Access Catalogue. DBIT. 18, 5; 1998, 3-8.

34. ASHEIM (Lester) and FRENWICK (Saral) Eds

Differentiating the media. 1975. University of Chicago Press, Chicago.

35. ASSOCIATION OF INDIAN UNIVERSITIES. Hand Book on Library and Information Science. 1997. AIU, New Delhi.
36. ASSOCIATION OF INDIAN UNIVERSITIES. Universities Handbook. 2000. AIU, New Delhi.
37. ASWORTH (Wilford). Ed. Hand Book of Special librarianship and Information work 1982. ASLIB, London.
38. AUBREY (Ruth H). Selected free materials for classroom teachers. 6th ed. 1978. Pitman Learning, Belnot, California.
39. AUDIO VISUAL POLICIES IN COLLEGE LIBRARIES. 1991. American Library Association, Chicago.
40. AUDIO VISUA HANDBOOK. 3rd Ed. 1954. Department of Public Instruction, Oklahoma.
41. BAHR (AH). Video in libraries: A status report 1979-80. *2nd* Ed. 1980. Knowledge Industries Publication Inc.
42. BANERJEE (SK). Electronic journals: A new era. IASLIC Bulletin. 44, 2; 1999; 61-65.
43. BANERJEE (BN). The rise of science and technology libraries. *Indian* Librarian. 19, 1; 1964. 12-22.
44. BANERJEE (Swapna) and CHAKARBARTY (Biplab). Digital Libraries: Some issues & perspectives. ILA bulletin. 34, 3-4; 1998-99; 60-63.
45. BASHIR AHMED. Information Communication Technology and Education. In GUPTA (Kalpana Das). Ed. Library practices for effective management: Papers of 47th ILA Seminar. 2001. ILA
46. BASU (ASHOK) and SARKHEL (JK). UGC-CDC recommendations on curriculum development in library and information science 1993: A Review ALSD. 42, 2; 1995; 67-78.
47. BHATIA (SK) and SURENDER (KAUR). Directory of

Libraries in Delhi. 1988. Reliance Publishing House, New Delhi.

48. BLAIR (PATRICIA) Treatment storage and handling of motion picture film. Lib Journal 17 (5) March 1, 1946.
49. BOARDMAN (Thomas H). A new style in audiovisual cataloguing. Educational Screen and audiovisual Guide 39, 3; March, 1960; 126-127.
50. BOWSER (Eiletoen) and KUIPER (John) Ed: a handbook of film archives. 1980. FIAF Secretariat, Brussels.
51. BOYLE (Deirdre). Expanding media. 1977. Oryx Press, Phoenix.
52. BRANCOLINI (Kristine) and PROVINI (Rick E). Video collection and multimedia in ARL libraries: changing technologies. OMS Occasional Paper 9. 1997. Association of Research Libraries, Washington.
53. BRITISH FILM INSTITUTE: RULES FOR USE IN CATALOGUING DEPARTMENT OF NATIONAL FILM LIBRARY. 1954. London.
54. BRIYANT (Eric Thomas). Music librarianship: a practical guide. 1959. James Clarke & Co., London.
55. BUKINGHAM (David). Watching media learning. 1990. Taylor and Francis.
56. BURKETT (Jack). Micro recording in libraries: a review of present practice. 19 57. Library Association, London.
57. BURKETT (J). Special Library and Information Service in the United Kingdom. 1973- Library Association, London.
58. BURTON (PF) and PETRIE (JH). Information Management Technology: A Librarian's guide. 1991. Chapman, London.
59. BUSHRA (CHARLES H) and HARTER (STEPHEN). Research Methods in Librarianship: Techniques and Interpretation. 1980. Academic Press, New York.

60. CABECAIRAS (J). The multimedia library: Material, selection and use. 1991. Academic Press, New York.

61. CABECIERAS (James). The multimedia library. 2nd Ed. New York, Academic Press, 1982.CURRAL (Henry FJ) Phonograph record libraries. 1963. Archer Books, Handen, Connecticus.

62. CAKEWELL (AE). Electronic documentation delivery system. Journal of Documentation 47, 1; 1991: 41-73.

63. CAROL (Goodson). Continuing challenge for librarians: meeting the needs of distance education. *MC Journal of Academic Media* Librarianship.4.1; 1996URL:http:// wings.buffalo.edu/publication smcjnl/v4ni/goodson.html

64. CATALOGUING RULES FOR NON BOOK MEDIA. *Unesco Bulletin* 26,1; 1972; 49-50,

65. CHADHA (Ravindra Kumar). Recent information technology for Indian libraries. *AGLIS Journal.* 11; 1995; 55-62.

66. CHINBALL (Bernard). The National Film Library and its cataloguing rules. The Jl. Of Documentation. 112; June 1955. 79-82.

67. COBOCEIRAS (James). The multimedia library. 2"1' Ed. 1982. Academic Press, New York.

68. COLLISION (Robert Lewis). The cataloguing arrangement and filing of special materials in special libraries. London, *ASLIB.* 1950.

69. COLLISON (RL). *Ed.* Libraries for television. Library World. 59, 781; July 1965; 3-7.

70. COLLISON (Robert L): Modem storage equipment and methods for special materials in libraries. 1955. Library Association, London.

71. DAILY (J. E.) Organizing non-print materials. 1986. Marcel Deckker, New York.

72. DALIP SINGH. Newspaper libraries. In JAIN (MK). Ed. Fifty years of library information service in India. 1998. Shipra, Delhi, 136-145.

73. DAY (Dorothy L) Film in the library. Library Trends 4, 2; October 1955,174-181.

74. DE KIEFFER (RE) and COCHRAN (Lee M): Manual of audiovisual techniques. 1966. Printice Hall, New Delhi.

75. DEOGAN (MS). Educating special librarians for 21st century. *Lucknow Librarian.* 20, 1; 1988; 18-22.

76. DHANIRAM. Art libraries their need and functions. *Indian Librarian.* 21, 3; 1966, 128-134.

77. DHIMAN (Anil Kumar). Impact of IT on library management. In GUPTA (Kalpana Das). Ed. Library practices for effective management: papers of 47th ILA Seminar. 2001. ILA, New Delhi. 191-202.

78. DHIR (BM). Types of media and its selection. 1987. TTTI, Chandigarh.

79. DOCUMENTATION RESEARCH AND TRAINING CENTRE. Associateship in Documentation. Prospectus and syllabus. DRTC, Bangalor.

80. DOVE (Jack A) the audiovisual : the availability and exploitation of non-print materials with special reference to libraries. 1975. Andre Deutsch, London.

81. DUBEY (Yogendra P). Artificial intelligence and future of libraries and information centres. In CHOPRA (HR). Eds. Library science and its facets V2. 1998. Ess Ess Publications, New Delhi. 20-29.

82. EDUCATIONAL FILM LOCATOR OF THE CONSORTIUM OF UNIVERSITY FILM CENTRE AND R. R. BOWKER COMPANY. 1st Ed. 1978. R. R. Bowker, New York.

83. EFFINGER (Carl). The filing and cataloguing of motion

picture film. Jl. Of the Society of Motion Picture Engineers 46, 2: February 1946-103-110.

84. ENCYCLOPAEDIA BRITANNICA FILMS, INC. How to run a film library.
85. ENRIGHT (BJ). Non-book/media materials in the library: a note. Library Association Record 72, 12; 1970; 368-69.
86. ERSTEIN (SB). Managing technology. *Library Journal.* 115, 6; 1990; 89-92.
87. ESCOLAR-SOBRINO (Hiplotito). Audiovisual materials and rural libraries. Unescp Bulletin 26, 1; 1972; 8-12.
88. ETHARAMA (S). Manpower planning in special libraries and information Centres. In Manpower planning for LIS in India: Papers of 17th IASLIC Conference. 1989, IASL1C, Calcutta, 1-15.
89. Evans (Hilary). Picture Librarianship. 1980. Clive Bingley, New York.
90. EVERSON (William K) Stocksots: potentiality of great creative importance, the new bolster inferior films. *Films in Reviews.* 4 (10 January, 1953; 15-20.
91. FISHBEIN (Meyer H). Progress on archival automation. *Indian* Archives. 32, 2; 1981, 59-68.
92. FLEISHER (Eugene) and GODMAN (Helen). Cataloguing audiovisual materials. 1980. Neal Schuman, New York,
93. FOCAL ENCYCLOPEDIA OF FILM AND TELEVISION TECHNIQUES. 1969. Focal Press, London.
94. FOTHERGILLS (Richard). Non-Book material in libraries. 1990. Clive Bingley, London.
95. FROST (Carolyn 0.) Cataloguing non-book materials: problems in theory and practice. 1983. Libraries Ltd, Littleton Colo.
96. GALVIN (Hoyt R) and SCRANTON (Jenne T). organization

of a library film service. Unesco Bulletin for Libraries 11, 11-12; Nov-Dec, 1957; 267-270.

97. GANGULY (SM). Towards an information society. *IASLIC Bulletin.* 40, 1; 1995; 17-20.

98 GAYASUDDIN. Library and information science education in the United States of America: An overview. ILA Bulletin. 24, 1; 1988: 37-47.

99. GIDLER (RS). Why pictures with words help the learners understand. Mediajn Education and Development, June 1985.

100. GILBERT (1) AND wright (J). Non-book materials: their bibliographic control. 1971. NCET Working Paper 6.

101. GOOD (WJ) and HATT (PK). Methods in Social Research: International students edition. 1983. McGraw Hill, New Delhi.

102 GOWTHAM (MS) and RAGHAVA (MC). Impact of new technologies on collection development and circulation in special libraries. LSSD. 19, 1; 1982; 21-53.

103. GRAHAM (Paul): Current developments in audiovisual cataloguing. Lib. Trends 34 1-2; 55-56.

104. GREENFELL (David). Standardization in film cataloguing. *Jl. Of* Documentation. 15, 20; June, 1959; 81-92.

105. GROVE (PEARCE) ed. Non-print media in academic libraries. (ACRL Publications in Librarianship No.34) Chicago, ALA, 1975.

106. GUIDE TO EDUCATIONAL MEDIA. 2nd Ed. 1877. ALA, Chicago.

107. GUIDELINES FOR AUDIOVISUAL SERVICES IN ACADEMIC LIBRARIES. Prepared by the Audio Visual Committee of the ACRL. 1968. American Library Association, Chicago.

108. GUIDELINES FOR AUDIOVISUAL SERVICES IN ACADEMIC LIBRARIES; prepared by the Audio Visual Committee, *C&RL New* 48, 1987;533-536

109. GUIDELINES FOR EXTENDED ACADEMIC LIBRARY SERVICES: A draft. *C&RL News* 58, 1997; 264-266

110. GULATI (Anjali). Knowledge Management: An information technology perspective. DBIT. 19, 6; 1999; 3-7.

111. GUPTA (RK). Directory of libraries in India. 1989. Atlantic Publisher and Distributor, New Delhi.

112. HAKA (RPS) and ARORA (Kamlesh): Electronic library: A myth or reality, ALSD. 42,4; 1995; 152-159.

113. HAMMER (Donald P). Ed. The information age: its development, its impact. Metuchen, 1976. Scarecrow Press, New Jersey.

114. HANDLEY (AM). The archival storage potential of microfilm,

115. HANDMAN (Gary) Ed. Video collection development in mutitype libraries: A handbook. 1994. Greenwood Press, Westport.

116. HARRISON (Helen P). Picture librarianship. 1981. The Library Association, London.

117. HFIELD (Edward T). Audio visual aids in the library. Library *Journal* 2 August. 1947; 181-82.

118. HICKS (W B) and TILLIN (A M) Developing multimedia libraries. 1970. Bowker, New York.

119. HICKS (Waren B). Developing multimedia libraries. 1970. R.R. Bowker, New York.

120. HIMMALFARB (Gertrude). Revolution in the library. The American Scholar. 66, 1997; 197-204.

121. HINTON (David B). Celluloid ivy; higher education in the movies 1960-90; 1960. Scarecrow.

122. HIRI (Abhijit) and SUNDER SINGH. Bibliographic databases and networks: Indian Scenario. NISSAT News Letter. 8,2: 1989; 3-16.

123. HNIEDERS (Sam). The Instructional Media Centre in the

Lincoln University Library. *MC Jl. Of Academic Media Librarianship.* 5, 1; 1997; 1-9

124. HOBON (Michi S). Sound recording cataloguing: a practical approach. Cataloguing and Classification Quarterly. 17, 2; 1990.

125. HORNER (John Leonard). Special cataloguing with particular reference to music maps serials and the multimedia computerized catalogue. 1973. Clive Bingley, London.

126. HUME (Margaret) Searching for Media in the online catalogue. MC Jl. Of Academic Media Librarinship. 3 (1) 1995 pi-18

127. INDIA UNIVERSITY GRANTS COMMISSION. Curriculum Development Committee on Library and Information Science. (Chairman: PN Kaula): A Report- 1992. UGC, New Delhi.

128. INDIA, MINISTRY OF EDUCATION, GOVERNMENT OF INDIA. Advisory Committee for Libraries. (Chairman: KP Sinha). A Report. 1959. Manager Publications, Delhi.

129. INDIA, PARLIAMENT. Information Management in the Parliament of India: Parliament Library and Reference, Research, Documentation and Documentation Service. 2000. Lok Sabha Secretariate, New Delhi.

130. INDIA, UNIVERSITY GRANTS COMMISSION. UGC Model Curriculum: Library and Information Science. (Convenor: Dr. C.R. Karisiddappa). A Report. 2001. UGC, New Delhi.

131. INDIAN ASSOCIATION OF SPECIAL LIBRARIES & INFORMATION CENTRES. Manpower planning for LIS in India: Papers of 17th IASLIC Conference. 1989. IASLIC, Calcutta.

132. INDIAN ASSOCIATION OF SPECIAL LIBRARIES & INFORMATION CENTRES. Education for special library

and information work: Papers of 16th IASLIC Conference. 1987. IASLIC, Calcutta.

133. INDIAN ASSOCIATION OF SPECIAL LIBRARIES *81*, INFORMATION CENTRES. Information technology products of 1990 and library and information centres: Papers of 20th IASLIC Conference. 1995, IASLIC, Calcutta.

134. INDIAN INSTITUTE OF TECHNOLOGY. Central library guide to library services: A Brochure for students. IIT, New Delhi.

135. INDIRA GANDHI NATIONAL CENTRE FOR THE ARTS. 'Kala Nidhi': A reference library: A pamphlet. IGNCA, New Delhi.

136. INDIRA GANDHI NATIONAL OPEN UNIVERSITY. Reaching the unreached: Technology enhanced learning. New Delhi, 2000.

137. INDIRA GANDHI NATIONAL OPEN UNIVERSITY: Profile 2000. New Delhi.

138. INDIRA GANDHI NATIONAL OPEN UNIVERSITY. School of Social Sciences. Programme Guide for Master Degree Programme in Library and Information Science. 2002. IGNOU, New Delhi.

139. INTER (Sheila) and STUDWELL (William E). Subject access to films and videos. 1997. Soldier Greek Press, Lake Crystal.

140. ITE (Herbert S). Managing the special library. 1984. Knowledge Industry Pub., New York.

141. JAIN (JK). Cosmic campus. Jl. Of Media and Technology for *Human Resource Development* 1 (2) 1987.

142. JAIN (MK) *Comp.* Handbook of Government Libraries. 1992. Shirpa Publications, Delhi.

143. JOSHI (SC) and PANDA (RN). Special libraries: An organization structure and staffing pattern. In MANGLA (PB). Eds. Fifty years of librarianship in India. 1983. ILA, Delhi. 201-206.

144. JOTWANI (D) and MEHTA (RD). Network of health sciences libraries in India: Role of National Medical Library. ILA Bulletin. 32,1-2; 1996, 17-19.

145. KALIA and SURENDER KUMAR. Directory of Scientific and Technical libraries in India. 1988. Reliance Publishing House, New Delhi.

146. KAPLAN (DON). Television and the classroom. 1986. Knowledge Industries Publications.

147. KARUNA SAHA. Information technology services and society. *AGLIS* Journal. 11; 1995; 20-25.

148. KAUL (HK). From printed bibliographies to online databases role of library network. In JAIN (MK) Ed. Fifty years of library and information services in India. 1998. Shirpa, Delhi, 261-273.

149. KENT (Alien). Ed. Encyclopaedia of Library & Information Science v. 28: Special Libraries and Special Libraries Association: 1980. Marcell Dekker, New York, 386-399.

150. KHAN (MM) Reprography for preservation of documents in library. In CHOPRA (HR). Eds. Library science and its facets 2v. 1993. Ess Ess Publication. New Delhi, 177-189.

151. KINDER (James S). Audiovisual materials and techniques. 1950. American Books.

152. KOTHARI (CR). Research methodology. Methods and techniques. 1987. Willey Eastern, New Delhi.

153. KRISHAN KUMAR. Library administration and management. 1987. Vikas Publishing House, New Delhi.

154. KUJOTH (JS) Ed. Readings in non-book librarianship. 1968. Scarecrow Press.

155. KUMAR (PSG) Some issues in education for librarianship in India. In Education for special library and information works: Papers of 16th IASLIC conference. 1987. IASLIC, Calcutta, 13-19.

156. KUMAR (PSG). Computerization of Indian Libraries. 1987. BR Publications. Delhi,

157. LADNER (SJ) and TILLMAN (HN). Using the Internet for references. Online 17, 1; 1993; 45-51.

158. LALLA (GT). Developing of media centres. *Jl. Of Engineering* Education 31 September 1989.

159. MAC CORMEC (Earl R). Visualization and information: computer images. The Southern Librarian, 40, 1990; 71-73.

160. MACER (P) and THOMAS (P). Browsing video content: Proceedings of the BCS HCI Group Conference, the Active Web. 1999. Staffordshire University.

161. MACER (P).and THOMAD (P). From video sequence to comic strip: Summarizing video for faster www access. British Computer Society, 1996; 16-18

162. MALWAD (NM). Information storage media and library effectiveness. In CHOPRA (HR). Eds. Library Science and its facets V2. 1998. Ess Ess publications. New Delhi, 227-242.

163. MASS COMMUNICATION RESEARCH CENTRE. Prospectus 1996-97. 1997. MCRC, New Delhi.

164. McGARRY (Charles J). The changing concept of information. 1981. Bingley, Bingley.

165. MEDIA STUDIES IN TRANSITION. AMFIT Conference Papers 1992. Association for Media, Film and Television Studies in Higher Education. 1993. NERDEN, Joseph Taft. A study of factors related to the use of motion picture film by public school teachers. 1953. Yale University.

166. MOHAMMAD YUSUF. Library & information science education in relation to professional manpower needs of special libraries of India. In CHOPRA (HR). Eds. Library science and its facets V2. 1998. Ess Ess Publications, New Delhi, 117-127.

167. NATRAJAN (M) and KALIYANI PERUMAL (R). Impact of new information technology on document provision and supply. ILA Bulletin. 24, 4; 1989; 214-220.

168. NERDEN (Joseph Taft). The study of factors related to the use of motion picture films by public school teachers. 1953. Yale University.

169. NEWSLETTER OF CONSORTIUM FOR EDUCATIONAL COMMUNICATION. 3, (10; October 1998. New Delhi.

170. NICEM INDEX TO EDUCATIONAL AUDIO TAPES. 5th Ed. University of Southern California, Los Angeles.

171. OLSON (Nancy B). Cataloguing of audiovisual materials. 4"' Ed. Media Marketing Group, Dekalb.

172. OLSON (Nancy B). 1996 update to cataloguing motion pictures and videorecordings. 1996. Soldier Greek Press, Lake Crystal.

173. OLSON (Nancy B). Cataloguing of audiovisual materials: a manual based on AACR2. 1981. Minnisota Scholarly Press, 1981. Mankoto Minn.

174. ORR (James M) Libraries as communication system. 1977. Greenwood Press, Westprot Connecticut.

175. PLANNING SCHOOLS FOR USE OF AUDIO-VISUAL MATERIALS, Nol Classrooms. 1953. National Education Association.

176. POOLE (Herbert) Academic libraries by the year 2000. 1977. R. R. Bowker, New York.

177. POWELL (L). A guide to use of audiovisual aids. 3rd Ed. 1973. Bacies Publication, London.

178. PRESTANO (Emanuel T) Ed. Audiovisual media in libraries: selected readings. 1977. Libraries Unlimited, Littleton, Colarado.

179. QUINLY (William J). The selection processing and storage

of non-print materials-aids, indexes and guidelines. Lib. Trends. 16 , 20: Oct. 1967; 274-80.

180. RAMAIAH (CK). Multimedia systems in libraries and their application. *DBIT.* 18, 6, 1998; 25-40.
181. RASTOGI (Satish). educational technology for distance education. 1998. Rawat Publication, New Delhi.
182. RAWTANI (MR) and ABDUL RASHID. Audio-Visual material: processing in Library science and its facets. New Delhi, Ess Ess Publications, 1998; 243-251.
183. REPORT FROM ALCTS MEDIA RESOURCES COMMUTE. 1999. American Library Association, New Oreleans.
184. RIDER (John Robert). A film selection aid for medium sizea academic libraries: a comparative study of academic film selection and evaluation procedures. 1987. Iowa State University, Iowa.
185. ROGER Jann V) and SAYA (Jerry D). Non-print cataloguing for multimedia collections: a guide based on AACR2. 2nd ed. 1987. Libraries Unilimited, Littleton, Colo.
186. RIECK (Donald Arthur). Video format influences and trends in university film rental libraries: An investigation of selection and evaluation procedures. 1987. Iowa State University.
187. SABIR HUSAIN (Mohd). Audio visual librarianship: a select bibliography 1961-66. Aligarh, Aligarh Muslim University, Library Science Department, 1967.
188. SABIR HUSAIN (Mohd). Emergence of audio visual material collection in libraries (Paper contributed to the 6th Seminar at Bangalore in 1970) Publidhed in IASLIC Special Bulletin No. 13 Part II. 87-88.
189. SAHI (Vikram Singh). Creation and preservation of digital resources. *University News.* 39, 12; 2001; 5-10.
190. SCHOLTZ (James C) and BARBARA (Santa). Developing

and maintaining video collections in libraries. CA ABC-Clio, 18989.

191. SCHRAMM (Wilbur) Big media little media. 1985. Sage Publications, London.

192. SHARAMA (S). Information management in the next millennium. In Information management in the context of fast emerging information society: Papers of 22nd IASLIC conference. 1999 IASLic, Calcutta. 225-238.

193. SON (Donald): A primer of non-book materials in libraries. 1958. Association of Assistant Librarians, London.

194. SONI (SK) and JAIN (PC). Interactive instructional television: a training system for tomorrow. *Jl. of ISDT* April 1989.

195. SONI (SK) Educational television and technical education: paper presented in ISTE's National Convention, 1988. Pune.

196. SONI (SK). Educational television in India: past present and future, a paper prepared for master of technical education programme. 1990. TTTI, Bhopal.

197. SUSHIL KUMAR. Directory of libraries in Delhi. 1973. Sterling, New Delhi.

198. SWANK (Reynard C). Sight and sound in the world of books. *Library* Journal V.78: Sept., 1953; 1959-64.

199. TANEJA (SK) CD-ROM in science and technological libraries with special reference to India. *ILA Bulletin.* 27, 3; 1991; 115-125.

200. TEAGUE (S John). Microfilm video and electronic media librarianship. 1985. Butterworths, London.

201. THOMAS (PETER). Browsing video over the web. *The Active Web*

202. UNESCO, DEPARTMENT OF MASS COMMUNICATION. International rules for cataloguing of educational, scientific and cultural films. Preliminary edition, 1956.

203. UNESCO. Reports and papers on mass communication. No. 35; 1962, 66.

204. UNSCO REPORTS AND PAPER IN MASS COMMUNICATION NO. 57: Script Writing for short films. 1969. Unesco, Paris.

205. USE OF AUDIOVISUALS IN EDUCATIONAL TECHNOLOGY FOR TECHNICAL EDUCATION AND TRAINING. New Delhi, McGraw-Hill Publishing Co., 1991; 123-128

206. VAN BOGART (John WC). Magnetic tape storage and handling: a guide to libraries and archives. 1995. The Commission on Preservation and Access, London.

207. WAGNER (RW). Film TV and video in the international encyclopedia of educational technology advances in education. Pergamon Press, 1989; 183-89.

208. WALIA (PK). Application of CD-ROM in libraries. In CHOPRA (HR). Eds. Library Science and its facets V2. 1998. Ess Ess Publications, New Delhi, 1998. 48-54

209. WITTICH (Walter Amo) and SCHULLER (Charles Francis). Audiovisual materials: their nature and use. New York, Harper and Brothers, 1957

210. ZIGARELL (James). The uses of television in American higher education. 1990. Praeger Publications, Greenwood.

INDEX

CD ROMs 17-18, 24-25, 104
Cinematography 12
Circulation 161-165
Computer Application 147-155
Content Development 192-193
Curriculum Development Committee Report 134
Cybermedia 28
Database Creation 155-161
Digital Communication 20-25
Document Imaging 176
Educational Films 83-87
    Acquisition 87-88
Educational Media
    History 33-38
    Growth 49-68
    Functions 54-56
    Organisations 56
Educational Television 125-129
Film Preservation 131-132
Film Production 99
Films 12
Filmstrip 71
Homepage 190
Information Networks 103
Information Sources 100-105
    Print 100
    Visual 101
    Electronic 103
    Audio 103
Information Systems 105-112, 115-118, 139-141
    Datasheet 110, 117
Internet 176
Internet 25-28
Internet Browsers 187
Internet Directories 183
Internet Service Providers 191-192
Intranet 185
Kits 72
Manuscript Preservation 166-172
Maps 72
Media 31-33
Media Libraries
    Collection Development 69
    Classification 90
    Cataloguing 92
    Indexing 95
    Subject Headings 96
Motion Pictures 13
Multimedia 24, 104
News Stories 114
Overhead Transparencies 75
Pamphlet 73

Paper
- History 2-8
- Manufacturing 5-6

Papyrus 2
Photography 9, 11
Programmed Instruction 74
Radio 9-10
Rough Cuts 114
Satellite Broadcasting 21-24
Search Engines 194
Slides 75
Stock Shots 112
Technology 31
Video 12, 44
Video Tape 74
Websites 194-